Open Innovation and Entrepreneurship

Gadaf Rexhepi • Robert D. Hisrich •
Veland Ramadani

Editors

Open Innovation and Entrepreneurship

Impetus of Growth and Competitive Advantages

 Springer

Editors
Gadaf Rexhepi
Faculty of Business and Economics
South East European University
Tetovo, Macedonia

Robert D. Hisrich
College of Business Administration
Kent State University
Kent, OH, USA

Veland Ramadani 🆔
Faculty of Business & Economics
South East European University
Tetovo, Macedonia

ISBN 978-3-030-16911-4   ISBN 978-3-030-16912-1   (eBook)
https://doi.org/10.1007/978-3-030-16912-1

This Springer imprint is published by the registered company Springer Nature Switzerland AG
The registered company address is: Gewerbestrasse 11, 6330 Cham, Switzerland

"Scholars Rexhepi, Hisrich and Ramadani bring together a helpful and informative collection of papers that speak to several of the key challenges to do with open innovation and entrepreneurship. The book segues across three fundamental themes: the consequences of partner choice and breadth, models of open innovation and their consequences for aspects of entrepreneurship, and the challenges of open innovation in different contexts (such as including firm age and size, and industry and economy). This book will no doubt serve as helpful resources for all those with an interest in open innovation!"

Mathew Hughes, Professor of Entrepreneurship and Innovation, Loughborough University

Open innovation is becoming more prevalent in entrepreneurial organizations across countries and it plays a key role in their growth. The renowned authors timely address this important topic in their book titled '*Open innovation and entrepreneurship: Impetus of growth and competitive advantages*'. This book will become a valuable resource for researchers, practitioners, educators, and students. I commend authors for their great contribution to the innovation and entrepreneurship fields.

Esra Mcmili, PhD, Associate Professor of Entrepreneurship, Margaret Van Hoy Hill Dean's Notable Scholar, University of North Carolina-Greensboro, USA

The *Open innovation and entrepreneurship: Impetus of growth and competitive advantages* book urges academics and practitioners alike to realize that no growth is a completely inner achievement and entrepreneurship creatively ignites it.

Massimiliano M. Pellegrini, University of Rome "Tor Vergata", Italy

Acknowledgment

We would like to thank all the respected contributors for making this volume achieve the required quality. Their cooperation, professionalism, and commitment shown through the entire process made it easy to manage. Without them, this book would never find its way to academic researchers, students, entrepreneurs, and policy makers.

The quality of this book was in the hands of our reviewers, who were selected professionals in the field of open innovation and innovation management. They all showed very high professionalism, cooperation, and objectiveness. Without the respected and appreciated reviewers, this book would not have the same value emphasizing the crucial aspects of the theoretic and practical insights provided by the contributors.

To our renowned colleagues who send us their endorsement and who also proved the high-quality standards required in this book. Considering that they are some of the most respected scholars in the field, their opinion also made this book more appreciated.

To the editor from Springer, Prashanth Mahagaonkar, and his great team, we are grateful for their thoughtful suggestions, support, and encouragement that were offered and well received.

Finally, to our families, friends, and colleagues, we must express our deepest appreciation. They are always helpful with their ideas and any other form that was asked. They stood by us since the very first beginning when the idea of this book was launched. Their support and motivation are always irreplaceable and necessary for each of us. We are very grateful to all of them.

Gadaf Rexhepi
Robert D. Hisrich
Veland Ramadani

Contents

Editors and Contributors

About the Editors

Gadaf Rexhepi is Associate Professor at South-East European University, Republic of Macedonia, where he teaches both undergraduate and postgraduate courses in the field of Management. His research interests include innovation, open innovation, strategy, family businesses and sustainability. He authored or co-authored around sixty research articles in different peer and refereed journals and ten text-books among which his later paper on Sustainable Development journal. He is part of many expert's team and have been invited by many organizations as lecturer and trainer. Dr. Rexhepi also has been engaged as advisor of the Minister of Economy in Macedonia. He served as a pro-dean for post-graduate studies 2012–2015. Recently he has been appointed as consultant for development of the Rector of South East European University. He serves on the editorial and review boards of several journals from in the field of entrepreneurship and management. He received the Award for Excellence 2016—Outstanding Paper by Emerald Group Publishing (Journal of Enterprising Communities: People and Places in the Global Economy).

Robert D. Hisrich is the Bridgestone Chair of International Marketing and Associate Dean of Graduate and International Programs at the College of Business Administration at Kent State University. Professor Hisrich's research pursuit is focused on entrepreneurship and venture creation: entrepreneurial ethics, corporate entrepreneurship, women and minority entrepreneurs, venture financing, and global venture creation. His interest in global management and entrepreneurship resulted in two Fulbright Fellowships in Budapest, Hungary; honorary degrees from Chuvash State University (Russia) and University of Miskolc (Hungary); and being a visiting faculty member in universities in Austria, Australia, Ireland, and Slovenia. Professor Hisrich serves on the editorial boards of several prominent journals in entrepreneurial scholarship, is on several boards of directors, and is author or coauthor of over 300 research articles appearing in journals such as *Journal of Marketing, Journal of Marketing Research, Journal of Business Venturing, Journal of Developmental Entrepreneurship*, and *Entrepreneurship Theory and Practice*. Professor Hisrich has authored or coauthored 45 books or their editions.

Veland Ramadani is an Associate Professor at South-East European University, Republic of Macedonia, where he teaches both undergraduate and postgraduate courses in entrepreneurship and small business management. His research interests include entrepreneurship, small business management, and family businesses. Dr. Ramadani is an Associate Editor of *International Journal of Entrepreneurship and Small Business (IJESB)*. He was engaged by the President of Republic of Macedonia, as a member of experts' committee to analyze the economical, technological, and juridical conditions for establishing techno-parks in the Republic of Macedonia. He also realized different training programs with the heads of departments in the Ministry of Economy. Recently, he was appointed as member of Supervisory Board of Macedonian Bank for Development Promotion. Dr. Ramadani received the Award for Excellence 2016—Outstanding Paper by Emerald Group Publishing (*Journal of Enterprising Communities: People and Places in the Global Economy*). His last book is *Entrepreneurial Marketing,* published by Edward Elgar.

Contributors

Hyrije Abazi South-East European University, Tetovo, Macedonia

David Adeyeye National Centre for Technology Management (Federal Ministry of Science and Technology), PMB 012, Obafemi Awolowo University, Ile-Ife, Nigeria

Biljana Angelova University "St. Cyril and Methodius", Skopje, Macedonia

Marcel Bogers University of Copenhagen, Copenhagen, Denmark

University of California, Berkeley, CA, USA

Ali Davari Faculty of Entrepreneurship, University of Tehran, Tehran, Iran

Abiodun Egbetokun National Centre for Technology Management (Federal Ministry of Science and Technology), PMB 012, Obafemi Awolowo University, Ile-Ife, Nigeria

Amir Emami Faculty of Management, University of Kharazmi, Tehran, Iran

Elena M. Gimenez-Fernandez Rey Juan Carlos University, Madrid, Spain

Inga Haase Department of SME Management and Entrepreneurship, University of Siegen, Siegen, Germany

Robert D. Hisrich College of Business Administration, Kent State University, Kent, OH, USA

Besnik Krasniqi Faculty of Economics, University "Hasan Prishtina", Prishtina, Kosovo

Lura Rexhepi Mahmutaj Faculty of Economics, University "Hasan Prishtina", Prishtina, Kosovo

Omolayo Oluwatope National Centre for Technology Management (Federal Ministry of Science and Technology), PMB 012, Obafemi Awolowo University, Ile-Ife, Nigeria

Amir Rahdari Tarbiat Modares University, Tehran, Iran

Veland Ramadani South-East European University, Tetovo, Macedonia

Gadaf Rexhepi South-East European University, Tetovo, Macedonia

Francesco Sandulli Universidad Complutense de Madrid, Madrid, Spain

Maruf Sanni National Centre for Technology Management (Federal Ministry of Science and Technology), PMB 012, Obafemi Awolowo University, Ile-Ife, Nigeria

Seyed Mohammadhossein Seyedi Faculty of Entrepreneurship, University of Tehran, Tehran, Iran

Open Innovation and Entrepreneurship: An Overview

Gadaf Rexhepi, Robert D. Hisrich, and Veland Ramadani

Abstract Open Innovation tends to be one of most growing field lately. Many excellent results from its implementation and the fast growing number of research in the field prove about its importance today and in the years to come. This book deals with open innovation and entrepreneurship from the perspective of how open innovation can help enterprises grow their businesses. Inside the book, there are many analysis and research dealing with open innovation and entrepreneurship and give more proves of its importance in helping enterprises to develop faster.

Introduction

One of the most challenges that all entrepreneurs face is the need to growth. Growth is part of all organizations, it implies continuous growth of sales, purchases, number of employees, profit and thus the normal growth of the enterprise (Hisrich and Ramadani 2017; Rexhepi and Srhoj 2018). Innovation is considered one of the main sources for enterprise growth (Rexhepi et al. 2013, 2018) but also finding the right strategy to implement this innovation (Rexhepi 2014, 2015). Most of the innovation that are part of the organizations are derived from inside the organizations. Traditionally innovation is viewed as taking place mostly within a single firm (Lee et al. 2010). However, many researches have proven that using innovation from inside the company (closed innovation) for entrepreneurial growth has its own limitations (Chesbrough 2006). Changes in our surrounding like in working patterns, increased labor division due to globalization, improved market institutions for trading ideas, and the rise of new technologies, as well as new trends such as outsourcing, agility, and flexibility requires from organizations to leave the closed

G. Rexhepi (✉) · V. Ramadani
South-East European University, Tetovo, Macedonia
e-mail: g.rexhepi@seeu.edu.mk; v.ramadani@seeu.edu.mk

R. D. Hisrich
College of Business Administration, Kent State University, Kent, OH, USA
e-mail: rhisric1@kent.edu

© Springer Nature Switzerland AG 2019
G. Rexhepi et al. (eds.), *Open Innovation and Entrepreneurship*,
https://doi.org/10.1007/978-3-030-16912-1_1

1

innovation approach and become network organizations (Huizingh 2011). Thus, researchers and practitioners need to rethink the design of innovation strategies in a networked world, they need to seek for new sources of innovation, which can be found in the new concept of open innovation.

Open innovation recently has become one of the hottest topic in innovation management; it is a rich concept, which can be used in many different ways inside the organizations. The open innovation concept tends to be one of the newest topic, and still it is not explored fully. Even though there are some, initial studies focus on successful and early adopters, which are based on case studies and some quantitative studies, which showed that it has been a valuable concept for so many firms and in so many contexts (Huizingh 2011).

Open innovation models explain that organizations can use many sources of knowledge and new ideas for a firm's innovation and invention activities, including customers, rivals, academics, and firms in unrelated industries (West and Gallagher 2006). Chesbrough (2006, p. xxiv), argues that open innovation is "a paradigm that assumes that firms can and should use external ideas, as well as internal ideas and internal and external paths to market, as the firms look to advance their technology". Open innovation means that ideas emerge and can be commercialized from inside or outside the firm (Dahlander and Gann 2010). Openness means that a single organization cannot innovate in isolation; it has to engage with different types of organizations so that it can acquire new ideas and resources, it emphasizes that firms' boundaries where ideas, resources and individuals flow in and out of organizations (Dahlander and Gann 2010). This collaboration has produced innovative product such as the Linux operating system, Firefox web browser, and the Apache web server (West and Gallagher 2006). These cooperations are better understood through models of innovation explained in this book.

Open innovation concept has many advantages; such as (Dahlander and Gann 2010): (a) It reflects social and economic changes in working patterns, where professionals seek portfolio careers rather than a job-for-life with a single employer. Firms therefore need to find new ways of accessing talent that might not wish to be employed exclusively and directly; (b) Globalization has expanded the extent of the market that allows for an increased division of labour; (c) Improved market institutions such as intellectual property rights (IPR), venture capital (VC), and technology standards allow for organization to trade ideas; (d) New technologies allow for new ways to collaborate and coordinate across geographical distances.

Nevertheless, most of the research done related to open innovation have been studied mainly in high-tech, multinational enterprises, but they are used also by small-and medium-sized enterprises (Van de Vrande et al. 2009). However, there are differences in the potential used from big companies and small and medium sized enterprises. Van de Vrande et al. (2009), found that medium-sized firms are on average more heavily involved in open innovation than their smaller counterparts are. It was also found that SMEs pursue open innovation primarily for market-related motives such as meeting customer demands or keeping up with competitors. Even though that this topic is still ongoing, more and more researches are proving the potential of open innovation for SMEs, indicating networking as one the most effective way to increase the open innovation capacity among SMEs (Lee et al. 2010). Researcher also need to address issues such is the organizational dynamics of university firm relationships, which remains under-researched (Perkmann and Walsh 2007). The success of the use of open innovations depends from capacity of one organization and its preparations. Organizations that tend to use open innovation need to address three fundamental challenges for organizations in applying it in the organizations: finding creative ways to exploit internal innovation, incorporating external innovation into internal development, and motivating outsiders to supply an ongoing stream of external innovations (West and Gallagher 2006).

This book will represent a picture of how open innovation serves as an impetus of growth of entrepreneurial businesses and way of creating of competitive advantage. It will provide major theoretical and empirical evidence that relates with open innovation and entrepreneurship and how it can help enterprises grow and create competitive advantage. This volume includes contributions of highly reputed authors and experts in the field of open innovation and entrepreneurship, specially written for the purposes of this book. Taking into consideration that such book is not available in the market and no author has treated the above-mentioned topics in this way, this book would be very welcomed by researchers who are interested to know more about open innovation and entrepreneurship and how it can help enterprises grow their businesses and create competitive advantage.

Therefore, this book includes chapters that analyze the theoretical content of open innovation and entrepreneurship, and it includes a lot of empirical analyses and cases. More specifically, the book will focus on research dealing with the following issues:

- Diversity of cooperation partners and its affects in start-ups' innovation performance: An analysis of the role of cooperation breadth in open innovation
- Investigating the effect of inbound and outbound open innovation on discovery and exploiting of entrepreneurial opportunities
- How knowledge service firms absorb and compete for innovating?
- Open innovation models for increased innovation activities and enterprise growth.
- Open innovation in a start-up firm
- Open Innovation: Challenges of integrating new forms of innovation in SMEs
- Open innovation's barriers in creating idea's explosion
- The role of industry and economic context in open innovation

The editors intend to bring with this book a significant value to open innovation and entrepreneurship researchers, policy-makers and entrepreneurs. All chapters suitable for publication in this book are double blind reviewed, following the publisher's review process guidelines.

Overview of Book Chapters

The book 'Open innovation and Entrepreneurship: Impetus of growth and competitive advantages' is consisted of nine chapters. This first chapter was focused on providing an overview of open innovation and entrepreneurship and their role to the development of the companies.

Elena M. Gimenez-Fernandez, Marcel Bogers and Francesco Sandulli in Chap. 2, titled as *"How the diversity of cooperation partners affects startups' innovation performance: An analysis of the role of cooperation breadth in open innovation"* study the relationship between the diversity of partners that a start-up cooperates with and its innovation performance. Based on data from the Spanish Innovation Technology Panel (PITEC) from 2004 to 2013, they found that start-ups benefit more than incumbent firms do from cooperation breadth. In addition, their study found that this effect is stronger for high-tech start-ups in particular. Their study is a great contribution to the link between open innovation and entrepreneurship, it advances our knowledge on the role of breadth as a mechanism to integrate heterogeneous knowledge and access to complementary assets, and it sheds light on some of the contingencies in terms of which types of start-ups will benefit most.

Chapter 3, *"Open innovation models for increased innovation activities and enterprise growth."* is contributed by Gadaf Rexhepi, Hyrije Abazi-Alili, Amir Rahdari, Biljana Angelova the purpose of this chapter is to present a literature review related to open innovation and its models and how they affect enterprise growth. This book chapter represents the importance of innovation and open innovation to the development of enterprises. Special emphasize in this chapter is given to the evolution of open innovation models and how this has influence enterprises' effectiveness and efficiency, which further influence enterprises' growth.

Chapter 4 *"Investigating the effect of inbound and outbound open innovation on discovery and exploiting of entrepreneurial opportunities"* is contributed by Ali Davari, Amir Emami and Seyed Mohammadhossein Seyedi. They investigated the effect of inbound and outbound open innovation on the discovery and exploitation of entrepreneurial opportunities. The authors selected nine indicators for inbound and six indicators for outbound open innovation were selected. The sample is consisted of 83 small and medium sized enterprises that operate in the IT sector. They concluded that only a small number of inbound and outbound open innovation indicators have a positive impact on the discovery and exploitation of entrepreneurial opportunities.

Abiodun Egbetokun, Omolayo Oluwatope, David Adeyeye and Maruf Sanni authored Chap. 5—*"The role of industry and economic context in open innovation"*. Authors, based on multiple research streams that includes economics of innovation and development economics, developed and tested several hypotheses on sectoral differences and the role of the economic context. They concluded that a wider range of innovation obstacles implies broader external search and more intense obstacles require deeper search.

Chapter 6, titled *"Open innovation: challenges of integrating new forms of innovation in SMEs"* is written by Inga Haase. Using qualitative empirical case study, the author addresses the question: How do small enterprises handle the process of integrating open innovation initiatives into the company? The author concludes that three main areas are essential for the integration of an open innovation initiative in SMEs: communication, culture, and innovation, which led to the identification of four important factors, such as technical operational management competence, operational-social management competence, social-technical management competence and the factor "words and deeds".

Chapter 7, *"Open innovation in a start-up firm"* contributed by Lura Rexhepi Mahmutaj and Besnik Krasniqi explores the impact of open innovation in the start-up firm growth. The research approach in this book chapter is based on a single case study by interviewing an innovative firm in Kosovo, Formon 3D Printer. The empirical findings show a low level of open innovation with establishment of Formon 3D. They managed to collaborate with only one professor of University of Prishtina at the beginning stage. They discuss the challenges of effective collaboration of entrepreneurs and partners' commitment to supporting firm growth.

Conclusion

The editors and the contributors of this book hope that this volume brings an attractive and significant contribution to the emerging field of open innovation and entrepreneurship and how open innovation can help companies' growth. The book provides many new researches and new results, which brings additional data and information on open innovation and their positive impact in providing new growth opportunities of companies. This book also provides new research about the possibilities of the use of open innovation in small and medium enterprises also and how this can be improved in the future. We strongly believe that this book will be used as a useful outlet for further research toward better understanding of the importance of open innovation to the development and growth of companies.

References

Chesbrough, H. W. (2006). The era of open innovation. *Managing Innovation and Change, 127*(3), 34–41.

Dahlander, L., & Gann, D. M. (2010). How open is innovation? *Research Policy, 39*(6), 699–709.

Hisrich, D. R., & Ramadani, V. (2017). *Effective entrepreneurial management*. Cham: Springer.

Huizingh, E. K. (2011). Open innovation: State of the art and future perspectives. *Technovation, 31*(1), 2–9.

Lee, S., Park, G., Yoon, B., & Park, J. (2010). Open innovation in SMEs—An intermediated network model. *Research Policy, 39*(2), 290–300.

Perkmann, M., & Walsh, K. (2007). University–industry relationships and open innovation: Towards a research agenda. *International Journal of Management Reviews, 9*(4), 259–280.

Rexhepi, G. (2014). Use the right strategy and grow. *ACRN Journal of Entrepreneurship Perspectives, 3*(1), 19–29.

Rexhepi, G. (2015). Entering new markets: Strategies for internationalization of family businesses. In *Family businesses in transition economies* (pp. 293–303). Cham: Springer.

Rexhepi, G., & Srhoj, S. (2018). Strategy as an ever evolving road to success of growing enterprises. *World Review of Entrepreneurship, Management and Sustainable Development, 14*(3), 333–347.

Rexhepi, G., Kurtishi, S., & Bexheti, G. (2013). Corporate social responsibility (CSR) and innovation–the drivers of business growth? *Procedia-Social and Behavioral Sciences, 75,* 532–541.

Rexhepi, G., Bexheti, A., Ibraimi, S., & Kurtishi-Kastrati, S. (2018). The importance of intellectual capital in the selection of global marketing strategies: Evidence from family businesses in Macedonia. *International Journal of Transitions and Innovation Systems, 6*(2), 108–117.

Van de Vrande, V., De Jong, J. P., Vanhaverbeke, W., & De Rochemont, M. (2009). Open innovation in SMEs: Trends, motives and management challenges. *Technovation, 29*(6–7), 423–437.

West, J., & Gallagher, S. (2006). Challenges of open innovation: The paradox of firm investment in open-source software. *R&D Management, 36*(3), 319–331.

Gadaf Rexhepi is Associate Professor at South-East European University, Republic of Macedonia, where he teaches both undergraduate and postgraduate courses in the field of Management. His research interests include innovation, open innovation, strategy, family businesses and sustainability. He authored or co-authored around sixty research articles in different peer and refereed journals and ten text-books among which his later paper on Sustainable Development journal. He is part of many expert's team and have been invited by many organizations as lecturer and trainer. Dr. Rexhepi also has been engaged as advisor of the Minister of Economy in Macedonia. He served as a pro-dean for post-graduate studies 2012–2015. Recently he has been appointed as consultant for development of the Rector of South East European University. He serves on the editorial and review boards of several journals from in the field of entrepreneurship and management. He received the Award for Excellence 2016—Outstanding Paper by Emerald Group Publishing (Journal of Enterprising Communities: People and Places in the Global Economy).

Robert D. Hisrich is the Bridgestone Chair of International Marketing and Associate Dean of Graduate and International Programs at the College of Business Administration at Kent State University. Professor Hisrich's research pursuit is focused on entrepreneurship and venture creation: entrepreneurial ethics, corporate entrepreneurship, women and minority entrepreneurs, venture financing, and global venture creation. His interest in global management and entrepreneurship resulted in two Fulbright Fellowships in Budapest, Hungary; honorary degrees from Chuvash State University (Russia) and University of Miskolc (Hungary); and being a visiting faculty member in universities in Austria, Australia, Ireland, and Slovenia. Professor Hisrich serves on the editorial boards of several prominent journals in entrepreneurial scholarship, is on several boards of directors, and is author or coauthor of over 300 research articles appearing in journals such as *Journal of Marketing, Journal of Marketing Research, Journal of Business Venturing, Journal of Developmental Entrepreneurship*, and *Entrepreneurship Theory and Practice*. Professor Hisrich has authored or coauthored 45 books or their editions.

Veland Ramadani is an Associate Professor at South-East European University, Republic of Macedonia, where he teaches both undergraduate and postgraduate courses in entrepreneurship and small business management. His research interests include entrepreneurship, small business management, and family businesses. Dr. Ramadani is an Associate Editor of *International Journal of Entrepreneurship and Small Business (IJESB)*. He was engaged by the President of Republic of Macedonia, as a member of experts' committee to analyze the economical, technological, and juridical conditions for establishing techno-parks in the Republic of Macedonia. He also realized different training programs with the heads of departments in the Ministry of Economy. Recently, he was appointed as member of Supervisory Board of Macedonian Bank for Development Promotion. Dr. Ramadani received the Award for Excellence 2016—Outstanding Paper by Emerald Group Publishing (*Journal of Enterprising Communities: People and Places in the Global Economy*). His last book is *Entrepreneurial Marketing,* published by Edward Elgar.

How the Diversity of Cooperation Partners Affects Startups' Innovation Performance: An Analysis of the Role of Cooperation Breadth in Open Innovation

Elena M. Gimenez-Fernandez, Marcel Bogers, and Francesco Sandulli

Abstract This study examines the relationship between the diversity of partners that a startup cooperates with and its innovation performance. Open innovation is important for startups as they need to open their boundaries to overcome the liabilities of newness. Based on data from the Spanish Innovation Technology Panel (PITEC) from 2004 to 2013, we find that startups benefit to a greater extent than incumbent firms from cooperation breadth. Moreover, we find that this effect is stronger for high-tech startups in particular. We therefore conclude that the breadth of cooperation partners plays an important role in knowledge exploration and exploitation in startups. This study contributes to the link between open innovation and entrepreneurship, it advances our knowledge on the role of breadth as a mechanism to integrate heterogeneous knowledge and access to complementary assets, and it also sheds light on some of the contingencies in terms of which types of startups will benefit most.

Introduction

From a Schumpeterian point of view, startups are a key driver in the production of innovation and economic change. For developing innovations and new knowledge combinations it is essential to acquire external scientific, technological and

---

This chapter shares a major portion of its content from the dissertation 'The role of cooperation breadth as a strategy for innovation: a study of openness in Spanish startups' written by Elena M. Giménez Fernández and submitted to Complutense University of Madrid.

E. M. Gimenez-Fernandez (✉)
Rey Juan Carlos University, Madrid, Spain
e-mail: elena.gimenez@urjc.es

M. Bogers
University of Copenhagen, Copenhagen, Denmark

University of California, Berkeley, CA, USA

F. Sandulli
Universidad Complutense de Madrid, Madrid, Spain

© Springer Nature Switzerland AG 2019
G. Rexhepi et al. (eds.), *Open Innovation and Entrepreneurship*,
https://doi.org/10.1007/978-3-030-16912-1_2

entrepreneurial knowledge (Spender et al. 2017). Evolutionary economics focusses on the role of new knowledge creation that explains the creation and survival of new firms (Audretsch 1995). Startups need to create routines to generate new knowledge, a process which is explained by organizational learning theories (i.e. Sapienza et al. 2006). In this content, one of the main cornerstones of entrepreneurial research is the study of organizational learning processes as a key driver for startups' success. Organizations may learn from direct experience or from the experience of others (Levitt and March 1988). Since compared to other organizations startups are characterized by newness, the potential to retrieve lessons from their own history would be limited. For this reason, organizational learning in startups results in the development of new products from the acquisition and absorption of external technological knowledge (Almeida et al. 2003). This paper explores this second learning context by studying how startups may benefit from defining external knowledge source strategies. Among all the external knowledge strategies, cooperating with a diversity of partners might bring more heterogeneous knowledge to startups with potential for new recombinations (Pangarkar and Wu 2013).

Startups' endowment of resources and capabilities is different from that of incumbent firms. Startups face two huge problems: smallness and newness (Stinchcombe 1965), so they lack human, financial and complementary assets to complete their innovation processes. However, they have inventive capabilities since they are flexible and do not restrict to a particular way of doing things (Katila and Shane 2005). On this basis, startups need external sources to overcome their liabilities, but they are also prospective partners for incumbent firms. Existing open innovation research has mainly focused on the role of openness for large and established companies (Gassmann et al. 2010), with scant papers focused on small and medium firms (SMEs) (Brunswicker and Vanhaverbeke 2015) and startups (Alberti and Pizzurno 2017; Criscuolo et al. 2012; Segers 2015; Spender et al. 2017; Usman and Vanhaverbeke 2017). Startups are different from SMEs and large firms because they are bounded by the liability of newness (Usman and Vanhaverbeke 2017), so more research that analyses the particularities of startups is needed. Among the studies that have addressed the differences between startups and incumbent firms, Criscuolo et al. (2012) differentiated between services and manufacturing firms, and they found that in services, startups are more innovative than incumbent firms, while in manufacturing, there are no significant differences; Katila and Shane (2005) found that startups contribute to markets where diversity in approaches to innovation is high, while incumbent firms operate in markets where innovation routines are standardised. Gimenez-Fernandez and Beukel (2017) evidenced that startups have a higher rate of cooperation breadth and innovation performance, but they did not investigate inference relationships. Although these studies provide some insights to understand the differences in innovation activities between startups and incumbent firms, they do not explain how startups take advantage of cooperating with a diversity of external sources for their innovation outcome. This research fills that research gap.

The differences in extracting the benefits from external sources could also be dependent on some contingencies, such as the industrial sector in which the firm operates. The industry is the most obvious external characteristic that might affect the effectiveness of open innovation (Huizingh 2010). Theoretically, technology intensive sectors generate more opportunities and boost the use of external sources and open innovation strategies (Schroll and Mild 2011; von Tunzelmann and Acha 2006). However, some scholars argue that when other factors are taken into account, for example, firm size, it is not clear that openness is more important for intensive technology sectors (Tether 2002; Chesbrough and Crowther 2006). To contribute to this research gap, this study analyses whether startups operating in knowledge-intensive industries benefit to a greater extent from a diversity of external sources.

We test our model on a panel dataset from the Spanish Technological Innovation Panel database (PITEC), collected by the Spanish National Statistics Institute (INE). Our results show that cooperation breadth draws an inverted-U shape with the innovation performance, and these effects are steepening in the case of startups. The liabilities of smallness and newness allow startups to benefit to a greater extent from external breadth. In particular, startups in high-tech sectors are those that can benefit the most from cooperation breadth because they are highly dependent on external resources.

This paper contributes to the literature in several ways. First, it provides for an advance in the integration of open innovation with entrepreneurship theory. Scholars have underlined the important role of external actors for startups' innovation processes and have highlighted the need for future studies to focus on them (Bogers et al. 2017; Brunswicker and Van De Vrande 2014; Eftekhari and Bogers 2015). To our knowledge no previous studies have analysed whether startups benefit to a greater extent from cooperation breadth for innovation performance. The smallness and newness liabilities that startups suffer, rather than being a limitation, are an incentive for openness. Our findings pose the nature of breadth in two ways, first, as a mechanism to integrate heterogeneous external knowledge, so startups' dynamic are more important than having an extended knowledge base, and second to provide complementary assets. Second, the study contributes to understanding of the contingencies on open innovation strategies. We provide a deep analysis of the relationship between knowledge-intensive industries and openness, providing evidence that the steepening effect of cooperation breadth in high-tech sectors is kept when startups are considered. Third, this study further contributes to the empirical literature because it uses panel data, stretching over a 10 year period.

The remainder of this paper is structured as follows. In the next section we review the theoretical background and develop our hypotheses. The third section describes the methodology and in the fourth section we present the statistical tools used and the results of our analyses. We then discuss our findings. Finally, we conclude with implications and directions for future research.

Conceptual Background and Hypothesis

Conceptual Background

The knowledge-based view literature has linked knowledge management to firms' innovation performance (Bengtsson et al. 2015). Open innovation literature highlights that internal knowledge must be combined with external knowledge to enhance firms' innovation performance (e.g. Berchicci 2013; Chesbrough 2006; Santamaría et al. 2009). Two key characteristics of external knowledge search are uncertainty and irreversibility (Nelson and Winter 1982). Firms need to be accurate in defining specific routines to determine the direction of their cooperation activities. Since external cooperation implies highly uncertain outcomes, firms may mitigate the risk associated to external cooperation by diversifying knowledge sources. In this sense, among the different routines that explain successful inbound open innovation strategies, open innovation research has shown the relevance of an efficient degree of sources breadth. Laursen and Salter (2014) defined cooperation breadth as the number of different types of sources with which a firm cooperates, such as suppliers, customers, competitors, consultants, universities, research centres, etc. Each type of external source have a different knowledge base that combined with the own base of knowledge of the firm, result in a different knowledge recombination (Teece 1986). External sources also differ in the facility to access that knowledge (Un et al. 2010) and in the strength of this interaction (Brunswicker and Vanhaverbeke 2015). Even if firms may benefit from cooperating with diverse external sources, transaction costs and the need for specific capabilities to obtain and exploit heterogeneous knowledge may constrain the returns to excessively diversified sources (Laursen and Salter 2006). Empirical literature has evidenced that the effect of external breadth on the innovation performance might be positive (Chesbrough and Appleyard 2007; Leiponen and Helfat 2010; Zobel 2013), inverted-U shaped (Laursen and Salter 2006; Leeuw et al. 2014; Oerlemans et al. 2013), or even negative (Bengtsson et al. 2015).

Startups depend on those knowledge flows. There is a consensus among literature from different theoretic perspectives that openness to external sources (e.g. cooperation strategies) are critical to startups. The resource based view of the firm (RBV) suggests that startups overcome their liabilities of smallness and newness (Stinchcombe 1965) by using their networks to acquire the resources that they lack (Bhalla and Terjesen 2013; Eisenhardt and Schoonhoven 1996; Gruber et al. 2010, 2013; Haeussler et al. 2012; Neyens et al. 2010; Pangarkar and Wu 2013). In his literature review paper, Hayter (2013) brings four theoretical frameworks—network approach, social capital perspective, relational view perspective, and knowledge spillover perspective- to evidence that networks and networks characteristics provide important resources to entrepreneurial performance. First, the network approach proposes that founders use their personal network of professional contacts to acquire information and resources that are of critical importance to and enhance firm performance (Larson and Starr 1993). Second, with regard to the social capital perspective (e.g. Gulati et al. 2000; Hoang and Antoncic 2003; Walker et al. 1997), it highlights the value of specific relationship ties and characteristics of the network overall, underlining the role of the network density and trust on partners to transmit knowledge between partners and enhance firm exchanges and entrepreneurial performance (Coleman 1988). Third, the relational view perspective argues that external relationships are a source of 'relational rents' and competitive advantage in terms of specific assets, knowledge-sharing routines, complementary resources or capabilities, and effective governance (Dyer and Singh 1998). Fourth, the knowledge spillover perspective emphasizes the role of external relationships in knowledge dissemination and economic growth (Cockburn and Henderson 1998), and promotes firms clustering to tap knowledge spills (Audretsch and Lehmann 2005). Authors on this stream of literature (e.g. Acs et al. 2013; Audretsch and Lehmann 2005) consider that knowledge created endogenously results in knowledge spillovers which becomes a source for opportunity creation and exploitation by entrepreneurs. While these studies remark the relevance of external knowledge, little is known on the specific internal routines that startups deploy to search, capture, absorb and exploit external knowledge, which determine the potential benefits of open innovation for startups.

Startups and Cooperation Breadth

Startups can use the degree of cooperation breadth as a strategy to impact on innovation performance. External knowledge flows could be managed to meet the innovation outcomes of startups. The knowledge-based view points out two dimensions of knowledge management: exploration and exploitation (March 1991). Exploration is identified with knowledge generation (Spender 1992) and it refers to the idea that alliances are a vehicle for transferring and absorbing partner's knowledge as well as learning from the partner (Grant and Baden-Fuller 2004). Upon the above argument, startups could benefit more from knowledge exploration when engage in a diversity of cooperation activities because they need to access to more knowledge and learn from their partners.

First, the diversity of external relationships provides diverse knowledge insights, which foster the identification of more business opportunities. Exploring strategies involve the scout or search of knowledge in the external environment, where firms would be able to create new knowledge and find business opportunities (March 1991) that would eventually lead to increase the innovation performance. Scholars have stated that search strategies exert an impact on the innovation activities of firms (Katila and Ahuja 2002; Laursen and Salter 2006; Spithoven et al. 2013). Since startups existence depends on their ability to source novel information (Yu et al. 2011), cooperation breadth would bring them the necessary insights to discover business opportunities. The purpose of technology scouting into a diversity of sources is not to gather large sets of detailed information, but creating insights or awareness of technological opportunities and threats regarding patterns of change in external environment (Parida et al. 2012) to gain a competitive advantage at an early stage and to provide the technological capabilities needed to face these challenges (Rohrbeck 2010). In this sense, Alvarez and Barney (2001) stressed the importance for startups to be a continual source of innovation by developing an inventive capability that large firms cannot develop or imitate.

Second, exploration activities can be understood as a process of search, variation, experimentation and discovery (March 1991) that is used by startups. At the earliest stages, startups are usually engaged with proximate partners (Butler and Hansen 1991; Hite and Hesterly 2001; Lechner and Dowling 2003) because it is easier for them to reach acquaintances. However, to keep up with their innovation performance and find more diverse knowledge, they need to make a distant search that provides a different knowledge base with potential for recombinations of that new and unfamiliar knowledge with the existing knowledge (Nelson and Winter 1982). On this basis, Wadhwa and Kotha (2006) linked the exploration activities to distant search to explain firms' innovation processes, arguing that firms establish equity relationships with startups to explore for new opportunities. In the same way, startups use these relationships to identify opportunities with value creation potential. Hence, cooperation breadth involves a distant knowledge search that would let startups access different knowledge resources.

Regarding knowledge exploitation, it has been identified with knowledge application (Spender 1992) and it refers to knowledge share and access to exploit the complementarities between partner's knowledge bases, but maintaining the own distinctive specialized knowledge bases (Grant and Baden-Fuller 2004). Startups could benefit more from knowledge exploitation when engage in a diversity of cooperation activities because they offer commercial channels, perform as a sign of quality, bring complementary assets, and share the risks.

First, we have previously discussed that startups use external relationships to overcome their liabilities of smallness and newness (Colombo et al. 2006; Eisenhardt and Schoonhoven 1996). One of those limitations is the lack of market access or commercial linkages since startups are not visible and lack external legitimacy (Stinchcombe 1965). External cooperation partners become a source for complementary assets (Teece 1986) since they would provide the commercial assets that startups lack. Entrepreneurial literature has discussed that startups move from social networks to more strategic linkages, consists of professional and business partners (Butler and Hansen 1991; Hite and Hesterly 2001; Lechner and Dowling 2003). In this sense, firms can intentionally use their cooperation breadth to meet different types of partners to open paths to markets. In addition, a mechanism to get that market access is to engage with partners with commercial knowledge and reputation since external partners perform as a sign of quality and support for startups' legitimacy (Hoang and Antoncic 2003; Lee et al. 2012; Martinez and Aldrich 2011; Wang et al. 2012).

Second, grounding in the Resource Based View (RBV) and entrepreneurship literature, it has been argued that startups use external sources to overcome their financial and human needs (Bhalla and Terjesen 2013; Eftekhari and Bogers 2015; Haeussler et al. 2012; Pangarkar and Wu 2013). The diversity of partners is positive for startups' success because they would have a broader knowledge access. As startups grow, their resources needs change. Startups reallocate their resources according to their current needs. Cooperation breadth could be a way to answer to the change in resources needs. Partners could fill their resources gaps and provide complementary assets in a timely manner (Etemad and Wright 1999). Moreover, cooperation breadth provides insights of the market from different points of view, complementing the startups' understanding of the market condition to get a competitive advantage.

Third, researching, developing and commercializing new products might be a costly process, take a long time and be very risky for startups because of their smallness and newness liabilities (Stinchcombe 1965). Cooperation diminishes the risks and costs of the innovation process because they are split between the partners (Cassiman and Veugelers 2002). In the way that startups cooperate with diverse partners, they distribute their risks between several projects and share their costs with the collaboration partners, which decreases the risks of startups' mortality due to the failure of a project.

All in all, we consider that startups can benefit more than other firms from cooperation breadth because it helps them to overcome their liabilities of smallness and newness when explore and exploit external knowledge:

H1: Startups will benefit from cooperation breadth for their innovation performance.

High-Tech Startups and Cooperation Breadth

The effectiveness of cooperation breadth on innovation performance could be affected by the sector in which the startup operates. Startups, which are focused on bringing innovations to the market (Schumpeter 1934), could benefit more from openness in high-tech sectors because technology intensive sector generate more opportunities and boost the use of external sources and open innovation strategies (Schroll and Mild 2011; von Tunzelmann and Acha 2006).

On the one hand, in high-tech sectors, products are more complex and knowledge is more distributed, so firms need to allocate more resources for new product development. This necessity effect is more challenging in startups because they lack internal R&D resources (Eisenhardt and Schoonhoven 1996; Neyens et al. 2010; Stinchcombe 1965), so they will have a higher necessity to look for external agents with internal R&D capacities (Parida et al. 2012). On the other hand, in high-tech sectors firms are unlikely to encompass all the capacities needed to develop their innovations (Gassmann 2006), while startups enjoy from an inventive capability (Alvarez and Barney 2001; Neyens et al. 2010). As a result, startups in high-tech sectors will cooperate with larger firms to accomplish innovation projects since the complementary between firms generates situations of value creation (Alvarez and Barney 2001; Barge-Gil 2010; Bayona et al. 2001; Colombo et al. 2006; Tether 2002).

Technology intensive industries are featured by uncertainty that makes firms benefit from sharing risks with external partners. In the same way, these industries are characterized by technological turbulence or rapid technological development, making that awareness of the environment to be crucial (Barge-Gil 2010) and leading firms to open their innovation processes. Given the uncertainty and turbulence, larger firms opt to lean on internal knowledge to keep themselves under their technological trajectory (Almirall and Casadesus-Masanell 2010) and distinguish from their competitors (Toh and Kim 2013). On the contrary, startups are described as being more flexible (Hyytinen et al. 2015; Katila and Shane 2005) since they do not suffer from structural inertia (Criscuolo et al. 2012), which limits the ability of firms to introduce innovations. As a consequence, startups easily adapt to environmental changes because they are not restricted to a way of doing things, rather they can make adjustments in their organizations (Criscuolo et al. 2012; Katila and Shane 2005). Startups therefore are more flexible and they offer a fast answer when they have to readapt their search processes of external knowledge sources, balancing out the uncertainty inconveniences, which contributes to startups to benefit more from open innovation strategies.

In addition, in high-tech sectors is most likely to surge emergent markets. Emergent industries are characterized by the entry of new firms. In such industries, most of the knowledge is tacit and, hence, its access requires technological cooperation initiatives (Dussauge et al. 2000). Startups in these industries will tend to cooperate with partners in a higher propensity (Eisenhardt and Schoonhoven 1996). Since startups play a key role in this type of markets, and this industry requires to cooperate with external knowledge source, the positive benefits of cooperation breadth could be multiplied for startups. The diversity of partners will bring more resources, will reduce the costs and risks by sharing with other firms, and will help to legitimate the new market (Eisenhardt and Schoonhoven 1996), contributing to the innovation performance of startups.

Therefore, the lack of R&D resources, the inventive capability, the strength to adapt to environmental changes, and the emergence of new markets make startups to be prone to adopt open innovation strategies in high-tech sectors, and benefit more from cooperation breadth. Hence, we propose:

H2: The benefits of cooperation breadth for the innovation performance will be higher for startups operating in high-tech sectors.

Methodology

Sample

We test our model on a representative sample of Spanish firms from the Spanish Technological Innovation Panel database (PITEC), collected by the Spanish National Statistics Institute (INE), in collaboration with the Spanish Science and

Technology Foundation (FECYT) and the Foundation for Technological Innovation (COTEC). The database has a wide sector coverage including both manufacturing and service sectors, being representative of the population of Spanish firms. The survey is based in the core Eurostat Community Innovation Survey (CIS), whose method and types of questions are described in Oslo Manual (OECD 2005). CIS data has been used in numerous academic papers (e.g. Cassiman and Veugelers 2002, 2006; Escribano et al. 2009; Gimenez-Fernandez and Sandulli 2016; Grimpe and Kaiser 2010; Laursen and Salter 2006; Spithoven et al. 2011), and also applied in the context of startups (Colombelli et al. 2016; Criscuolo et al. 2012).

PITEC data are collected on a yearly base from 2003, and in 2004 and 2005 there were two enlargements of the sample. In addition, in 2004 PITEC introduced some important changes in the questionnaire, affecting variables related to cooperation with external sources for technology innovation, which are central variables in this study. Due to these limitations, this study will use data from 2004 to 2013 to test the hypotheses. Since we analyse the open innovation phenomenon, we only focus on firms that intended to have an innovation activity, even failed. In total, our sample consists of 76,764 observations from 11,085 firms.

Measures

Dependent Variables

In this paper we analyse the fact of being a startup on the relationship between cooperation breadth and innovation performance. A well-established proxy for innovation performance is product innovation (Belderbos et al. 2004; Faems et al. 2005, 2010; Laursen and Salter 2006; Nieto and Santamaría 2007). In the startup context, there is also strong support in literature for using product innovation as a proxy for innovation performance (Criscuolo et al. 2012) since it has been evidenced the role of startups in introducing new products to the market (Almeida and Kogut 1997). In the questionnaire firms are asked to assert what share of their sales can be ascribed to innovations new to the market. Hence, innovation performance is measured as proportion relative to turnover of new or strongly improved products that the company introduced to the market and that were new to the market.

Independent Variables

Cooperation breadth is defined as the number of different types of sources with which a firm cooperates (Laursen and Salter 2014). In the survey, firms are asked if they cooperated with the following sources in the last 3 years: suppliers, customers (private and public sector), competitors or other firms from the same activity field, consultants or commercial laboratories, universities or other higher education institutes, public or private research centres and technological centres. Following the methodology of Laursen and Salter (2006, 2014), the variable cooperation breadth is constructed as the addition of those seven cooperation partners. Each of the seven cooperation partners is coded as a binary variable, 1 if the firm cooperated with that partner, and 0 being no use. Subsequently, the seven types of cooperation partners are added up so that each firm gets a 0 when no cooperation agreements with any type of partner were taken, and 7 when it cooperated with all the different types of partners. Empirical literature has found mixed results regarding the linearity effect of external breadth on the innovation performance, evidencing a positive effect (Chesbrough and Appleyard 2007; Leiponen and Helfat 2010; Zobel 2013), inverted-U shaped (Laursen and Salter 2006; Leeuw et al. 2014; Oerlemans et al. 2013), or even negative effect (Bengtsson et al. 2015). To test the linearity of cooperation breadth, we included its square term.

Startups are new enterprises in the first stage of their operations trying to solve a problem whose solution is not guaranteed (Michelino et al. 2017). According to Blank (2010), a startup is a company, partnership or temporary organization designed to search for a repeatable and scalable business model. There is not unanimous definition of a startup, but literature highlights as a feature the age of the firm or the fact of being developing the business. Alberti and Pizzurno (2017, p. 53) defined a start-up as "a few-year-old business which is not yet established in the industry and in the market and could more easily fail". The survey asks firms if the firm is new creation or it was during the two last years, and we use this question to build the startup variable (Laursen and Salter 2006). Hence, startup is measured as a binary variable indicating whether the firm is of new creation. We create the interaction cooperation breadth and startup to test our first hypothesis.

Literature has discussed that firms operating in knowledge-intensive sectors are more prone to open their boundaries (Schroll and Mild 2011; von Tunzelmann and Acha 2006). We measure the intensive technology sectors through a dummy variable that indicates if the firm belongs to a high-tech sector (Luker and Lyons 1997). We follow the Spanish National Statistics Institute to determine the firms that operate in a high-tech sector. In particular, this classification considers that high-tech sectors are: pharmaceutical industry, computing material, electronic components, telecommunications, aeronautic and space industries, research and development services, and computing services. Since it is not clear whether the tendency to be more open in intensive technology sectors remains when considering other factors (Tether 2002; Chesbrough and Crowther 2006), we test the effect of cooperation breadth in high-tech sectors when the firm is a startup. For that purpose, we create a dummy variable indicating whether the firm is both a startup and it operates in high-tech sectors. We then create an interaction variable between cooperation breadth and startups operating in high-tech sectors.

Control Variables

In order to rule out possible alternative explanations to those formally hypothesized, the model includes the following control variables. First, as scholars consider internal R&D to be crucial for innovation (Lin 2003; Schmiedeberg 2008), and a proxy for absorptive capacity (Cohen and Levinthal 1990), we include firm's internal R&D efforts, measured as the proportion of its internal innovation expenses. Second, firms need to protect their innovations and deploy suitable appropriation strategies against imitation, as well as avoid intentionally or unintentionally allowing partners to collect all the benefits (Pisano 2006; Teece 1986). Literature has recognized the importance of having an appropriation strategy (Alkaersig et al. 2015; Gans and Stern 2003). Hence, we include a variable to control for the startups' formal appropriation strategy. This variable is built following Laursen and Salter (2014) methodology, where the addition of the different appropriation mechanisms that a firm uses generates the firm's 'appropriability strategy'. Our variable is therefore measured by the addition of the use of the four appropriation mechanisms—patents, trademarks, copyright, and design rights-. These items are binary variables, being 1 if the firm registered or applied it during the last 3 years, and 0 if it did not; and it gets the value of 4 when all the mechanisms were used by the firm, and 0 if it did not use any of them. Third, we also control for firm size as it has been argued to be relevant for firms' innovative behaviour (Berchicci 2013; Cassiman and Veugelers 2002). This variable is measured by the logarithm of the total number of employees. Fourth, we include a dummy variable to control if the firm belongs to a group because firms belonging to a corporate group could bring knowledge from the large corporation and being more innovative (Criscuolo et al. 2012). Fifth, we include as a control variable the scope of the market where the firm sells its products since it would increases the firm's market share. It is measured by the addition of the involvement in different markets: local, national, European, and other international markets (Laursen and Salter 2014). Finally, we have created dummy variables to control the possible bias of the observation year (Un et al. 2010; Wang et al. 2013). Controlling time-varying effects is necessary in a rapid changing environment such as technology and innovation, and to check if the economic crisis impact on results. A short description of the variables used to test the model and their references are included in Table 1.

Results

Table 2 reports the basic statistics of the variables used in the analysis. The percentage of sales of new products remains relatively stable over time, being higher in 2008–2010. It suggests that Spanish firms launched new products during the financial crisis to face it or as result of a previous innovation process that takes a couple of years to emerge. Indeed, the internal R&D expenses slightly decreased in 2008–2010. On the contrary, the use of external sources has increased over time. Our sample of startups is higher during the first years analysed due to the fact that PITEC is a panel survey, that is, it consists of repeated observations on the same cross section of economic agents over time. As a consequence the big sample of

Table 1 Variable description

Variable	Description	References
Innovation performance	Proportion relative to turnover of new or strongly improved products that the company introduced to the market and that were new to the market	Belderbos et al. (2004); Faems et al. (2005, 2010); Nieto and Santamaría (2007)
Cooperation breadth	Addition of seven cooperation partners: suppliers, customers (private and public sector), competitors or other firms from the same activity field, consultants or commercial laboratories, universities or other higher education institutes, public or private research centres and technological centres	Laursen and Salter (2006, 2014)
Startup	Dummy variable to indicate whether the firm is new creation	Laursen and Salter (2006)
High-tech	Dummy variable to indicate whether the firm belongs to a high-tech sector	Luker and Lyons (1997)
Internal R&D	Proportion of firm's internal innovation expenses	Lin et al. (2013); Schmiedeberg (2008)
Formal approp. strategy	Addition of the use of the four appropriation mechanisms: patents, trademarks, copyright, and design rights	Laursen and Salter (2014)
Size	Natural logarithm of the total number of employees	Audretsch et al. (2000); Berchicci (2013); Cassiman and Veugelers (2002)
Group	Dummy variable to indicate if the firm belongs to a firm group	Criscuolo et al. (2012)
Scope	Addition of the involvement in different markets: local, national, European, and other international markets	Laursen and Salter (2014)
Year	A set of dummy variables for the observation year	Un et al. (2010); Wang et al. (2013)

startups is introduced when the panel was created or with the two main enlargements (2004, 2005), but the minor enlargements over time introduce few startups in the database. From our sample of startups, 57% of them are firms operating in high-tech sectors.

Table 3 shows the correlation coefficients of the variables (except year dummies) and we can observe some significant correlations that reveals some interesting points. For example, startups relate positively to innovation performance, while the coefficient for larger firms is negative. Moreover, startups are also positively related to cooperation breadth. It suggests that the liabilities of smallness and newness make these firms to open their barriers, but it is not a limitation for innovation, rather a boost. High-tech firms are also positively related to the innovation performance and to cooperation breadth. None of the correlations are sufficiently strong to suggest multicollinearity problems. Before calculating the interaction terms, the variables were mean-centered to avoid multicolinearity issues (Van de Vrande 2013). In addition, we conducted a variance inflation factor (VIF) test. All the VIFs are lower than 10, and the average VIF is 2.06, indicating few problems of multicollinearity.

Table 2 Descriptive statistics

Year	Obs.	Inn. perform.	Coop. breadth	Startup	High-tech	Internal R&D	Formal appr. strat.	Size	Group	Scope
2004	7274	9.02	0.85	0.05	0.29	66.06	0.63	283.19	0.37	2.87
		(21.50)	(1.49)	(0.21)	(0.45)	(40.76)	(0.95)	(1220.55)	(0.48)	(1.05)
2005	9657	11.45	0.77	0.04	0.28	59.31	0.54	247.43	0.34	2.98
		(24.33)	(1.42)	(0.19)	(0.45)	(39.78)	(0.86)	(1100.58)	(0.48)	(1.12)
2006	9426	11.41	0.79	0.01	0.28	54.69	0.49	259.15	0.36	2.91
		(24.32)	(1.47)	(0.12)	(0.45)	(42.54)	(0.83)	(1186.94)	(0.48)	(1.07)
2007	8870	11.75	0.80	0.00	0.29	52.13	0.46	283.73	0.39	2.94
		(24.73)	(1.51)	(0.05)	(0.45)	(42.16)	(0.81)	(1372.70)	(0.49)	(1.06)
2008	8238	12.49	0.87	0.00	0.29	51.18	0.44	305.05	0.40	2.96
		(25.11)	(1.57)	(0.01)	(0.45)	(42.63)	(0.78)	(1530.17)	(0.49)	(1.04)
2009	7905	12.48	0.90	0.00	0.18	48.23	0.42	309.79	0.41	2.98
		(25.16)	(1.61)	(0.01)	(0.39)	(42.84)	(0.77)	(1591.57)	(0.49)	(1.04)
2010	7570	12.19	0.95	0.00	0.18	46.57	0.41	326.86	0.42	3.03
		(24.72)	(1.68)	(0.03)	(0.39)	(43.02)	(0.76)	(1598.32)	(0.49)	(1.04)
2011	6249	10.96	1.03	0.00	0.19	51.73	0.42	345.74	0.45	3.09
		(23.76)	(1.76)	(0.03)	(0.39)	(43.08)	(0.77)	(1654.55)	(0.50)	(1.03)
2012	5934	9.72	1.02	0.00	0.19	54.78	0.38	358.94	0.47	3.15
		(22.40)	(1.70)	(0.04)	(0.39)	(43.12)	(0.74)	(1769.52)	(0.50)	(1.01)
2013	5461	9.22	1.05	0.00	0.19	55.90	0.38	372.68	0.49	3.20
		(21.63)	(1.73)	(0.04)	(0.39)	(43.06)	(0.74)	(1834.45)	(0.50)	(1.01)

Note: Standards errors in brackets

Table 3 Correlation coefficients of major variables used in the model

	Inn. perform.	Coop. breadth	Startup	High-tech	Internal R&D	Formal appr. strat.	Size	Group
Coop. breadth	0.118							
p-value	0.000							
Startup	0.060	0.016						
p-value	0.000	0.000						
High-tech	0.123	0.120	0.076					
p-value	0.000	0.000	0.000					
Internal R&D	0.228	0.165	0.066	0.172				
p-value	0.000	0.000	0.000	0.000				
Formal Appr. Strat.	0.176	0.187	0.056	0.065	0.233			
p-value	0.000	0.000	0.000	0.000	0.000			
Size	−0.011	0.087	−0.014	−0.014	−0.045	0.028		
p-value	0.000	0.000	0.000	0.000	0.000	0.000		
Group	−0.018	0.119	−0.023	−0.037	0.001	0.031	0.163	
p-value	0.000	0.000	0.000	0.000	0.847	0.000	0.000	
Scope	0.092	0.077	−0.055	−0.097	0.258	0.199	−0.025	0.125
p-value	0.000	0.000	0.000	0.000	0.000	0.000	0.000	0.000

Note: This table omits the correlation coefficients of year dummies

This study uses longitudinal data from 2004 to 2013, so time-series effects can be considered. The nature of the variable related to the technology intensity sector in which the firm operates is almost unvarying because firms do not commonly shift between not related sectors, so keeping on high-tech sectors or low-tech, but not moving from high-tech to low-tech sectors. Hence, a fixed effect model would not be accurate. We consider whether random effects or pool data are more accurate. The Breusch-Pagan Lagrange Multiplier (LM) test to control for random effects indicates that random effects are relevant in our model ($\chi^2 = 27233.83$, p < 0.01). Hence, we will use random effects regressions.

To determine the statistical model, we first check if the assumption of normality of residuals in our model is satisfied. Since we find that residuals are not normally distributed, but it could exist a left censoring, we employ a censored Tobit model (Laursen and Salter 2006). This model was proposed by James Tobin (1958) to estimate relationships between variables when there is either left- or right- censoring or both left-censored and right-censored in the dependent variable. Moreover, to address the lack of normality of residuals, we assume a lognormal distribution for the residuals of the Tobit model (Laursen and Salter 2006). Hence, we introduce a latent variable, lnnewmer, as a logarithmic transformation of an observed measure of innovation performance, lnnewmer = ln(1 + newmer).[1] Our latent models would be as follows:

---

[1]Note: The lognormal transformation does not change the signs, nor the significance for the key variables' parameters in the subsequent estimations.

(#1) $y^*_i = Inn.\ Performance = \beta_0 + \beta_1 Coop.\ Breadth + \beta_2 Coop.\ Breadth^2 + \beta_3 Startup + \beta_4 Coop.\ Breadth*Startup + \beta_5 Coop.\ Breadth^2*Startup + \beta_6 InternalR\&D + \beta_7 Formal\ App.\ Strat. + \beta_8 Size(log) + \beta_9 Group + \beta_{10} Scope + \beta_{11} High\text{-}tech + \beta_{12} YearDummies + \varepsilon,\ \varepsilon \sim N(0,\ \sigma^2)$

(#2) $y^*_i = Inn.\ Performance = \beta_0 + \beta_1 Coop.\ Breadth + \beta_2 Coop.\ Breadth^2 + \beta_3 High\text{-}techStartups + \beta_4 Coop.\ Breadth*High\text{-}techStartups + \beta_5 Coop.\ Breadth2*High\text{-}techStartups + \beta_6 InternalR\&D + \beta_7 Formal\ App.\ Strat. + \beta_8 Size(log) + \beta_9 Group + \beta_{10} Scope + \beta_{11} High\text{-}tech + \beta_{12} YearDummies + \varepsilon\ \varepsilon \sim N(0,\ \sigma^2)$

The results of the random effects Tobit regressions can be found in Table 4. First, we estimate Model I, which contains the control variables (for reasons of space we do not include results from year dummy variables in the table); then Model II, which contains the independent and control variables of Hypothesis 1. In Model III we include the interaction term between cooperation breadth and startup. Model IV includes the independent and control variables of Hypothesis 2; and Model V also includes the interaction between cooperation breadth and startup in high-tech sectors.

We hypothesized that startups will benefit from cooperation breadth for innovation performance. Cooperation breadth draws a curvilinear relationship since we can observe in Model II that the parameter for cooperation breadth is significant and positive ($\beta = 0.387$, $p < 0.01$), while the parameter for its squared term is significant, but negative ($\beta = -0.031$, $p < 0.01$). Since we are testing the effect of being a startup over a variable that draws an inverted-U shape, we would confirm our hypothesis whether we observe a steepening of the curve. To test it, β_5 has to be significant and negative (Haans et al. 2016). In Model III, we observe that the coefficient for the interaction between cooperation breadth square and startups is significant and negative ($\beta = -0.083$, $p < 0.01$), confirming our Hypothesis 1. Figure 1 shows how the curve is steeped when the firm is a startup. We can also observe that the curve for startups is higher than that for non-startups. The graphic therefore provides support for Hypothesis 1.

In Hypothesis 2, we raised the question whether startups in high-tech sectors benefit more from cooperation breadth. Again, we are testing the effect of a variable—high-tech startups—over a variable that draws an inverted-U shape—cooperation breadth-, so we would confirm our hypothesis when we observe a steepening of the curve, which happens if β_5 is significant and negative (Haans et al. 2016). In Model V we observe that the coefficient for the interaction between cooperation breadth square and startups in high-tech sectors is significant and negative ($\beta = -0.088$, $p < 0.01$), meaning that startups in high-tech sectors benefit more from cooperation breadth than the rest of firms. Hence, we find support for our Hypothesis 2. Figure 2 graphically explains this effect. The curve for cooperation breadth is steepening in the case of high-tech startups. Note that for low levels of cooperation breadth, high-tech startups perform a lower innovation performance since they need external resources in their innovation processes.

Table 4 Tobit regression with random effects

	Model I	Model II	Model III	Model IV	Model V
Internal R&D	0.008***	0.007***	0.007***	0.007***	0.007***
	[0.000]	[0.000]	[0.000]	[0.000]	[0.000]
Formal appr. strat.	0.479***	0.427***	0.426***	0.428***	0.428***
	[0.017]	[0.017]	[0.017]	[0.017]	[0.017]
Size	−0.070***	−0.103***	−0.102***	−0.106***	−0.106***
	[0.017]	[0.017]	[0.017]	[0.017]	[0.017]
Group	0.151***	0.111**	0.111**	0.113**	0.113**
	[0.046]	[0.045]	[0.045]	[0.045]	[0.045]
Scope	0.279***	0.270***	0.270***	0.267***	0.267***
	[0.019]	[0.019]	[0.019]	[0.019]	[0.019]
High-tech	0.585***	0.519***	0.518***	0.517***	0.517***
	[0.048]	[0.047]	[0.047]	[0.048]	[0.048]
Year dummies	Yes	Yes	Yes	Yes	Yes
Coop. breadth		0.387***	0.385***	0.387***	0.386***
		[0.017]	[0.017]	[0.017]	[0.017]
Coop. breadth^2		−0.031***	−0.030***	−0.031***	−0.031***
		[0.004]	[0.004]	[0.004]	[0.004]
Startup		0.480***	0.639***		
		[0.109]	[0.124]		
Coop. breadth*startup			0.260**		
			[0.113]		
Coop. breadth^2*startup			−0.083***		
			[0.029]		
High-tech startup				0.254*	0.389**
				[0.141]	[0.162]
Coop. breadth*high-tech startup					0.313**
					[0.150]
Coop. breadth^2*high-tech startup					−0.088**
					[0.040]
Constant	−3.034***	−2.657***	−2.659***	−2.623***	−2.624***
	[0.097]	[0.097]	[0.097]	[0.097]	[0.097]
sigma_u	2.674***	2.598***	2.598***	2.599***	2.599***
Constant	[0.031]	[0.030]	[0.030]	[0.030]	[0.030]
sigma_e	2.282***	2.269***	2.268***	2.269***	2.269***
Constant	[0.011]	[0.011]	[0.011]	[0.011]	[0.011]
Log likelihood	−9.17E+04	−9.12E+04	−9.12E+04	−9.12E+04	−9.12E+04
No. of Obs	76,764	76,764	76,764	76,764	76,764
Left censored obs.	47,867	47,867	47,867	47,867	47,867
Wald-Chi2	2229.43***	3151.254***	3159.732***	3135.568***	3140.677***

Note: Standard errors in brackets

* p < 0.10; ** p < 0.05; *** p < 0.01

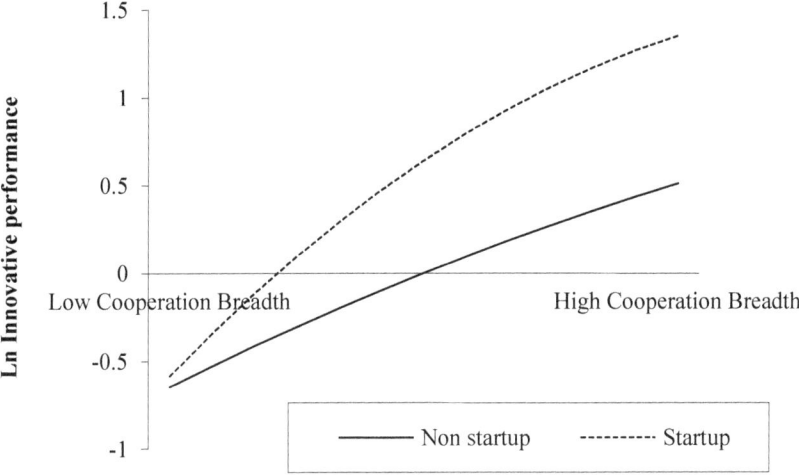

Fig. 1 Effect of being a startup on the relationship between cooperation breadth and innovation performance. Note: Graphic readjusted to the scale

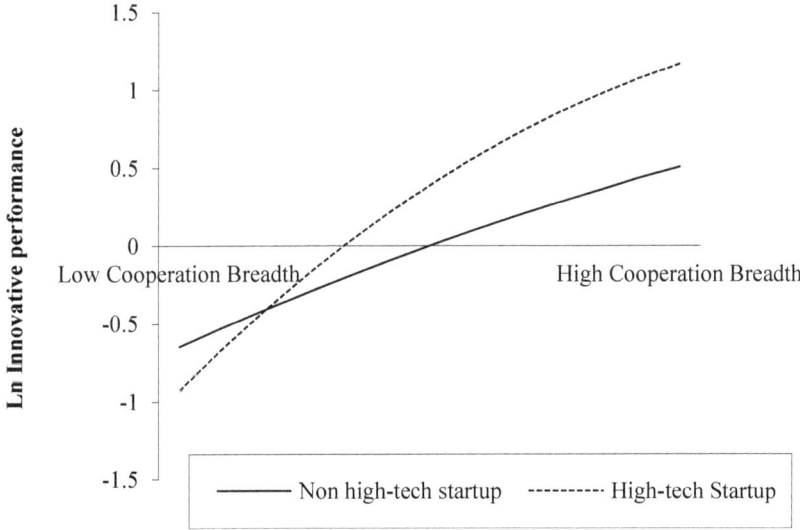

Fig. 2 Effect of being a high-tech startup on the relationship between cooperation breadth and innovation performance. Note: Graphic readjusted to the scale

From our control variables, we found evidence in all models of the positive impact of internal R&D expenses for innovation performance. We also found that the formal appropriation strategy is positively related to the innovation performance, so the use of intellectual propriety rights enhances innovation performance.

Firms with a greater market scope enjoy a higher innovation performance; and also firms operating in high-tech sectors. Finally, our models suggest that smaller firms have a higher innovation performance for products new to the market than larger firms.

We ran several further robustness checks (not included by the sake of brevity). First, we confirmed that our Tobit random effect models are robust to alternative estimations. We run a pooled Tobit regression and we found evidence for both hypotheses if the dependent variable is not transformed into a lognormal variable. Our control variables remained significant, except for the variable group, which had only weak significance in our model. We also run random effect OLS regressions, and they revealed same results than presented, but the group variable also turned insignificant (it presents the same sign that in Table 4). We also run cross-sectional OLS regressions, and our estimations support the results found in Table 4, again, except for the group variable.

Second, to check whether startups in all types of knowledge intensity sectors benefit to a greater extent from cooperation breadth, or this effect is only depicted by high-tech startups, we split the sample between high-tech firms and low- and medium-tech firms, and we found that the positive effect of being a startup keeps in both groups. Additionally, we ran a random effects Tobit regression where we include both high-tech and low- and medium-tech startups and their interaction with cooperation breadth. We found that the coefficient for the interaction term between cooperation breadth square and high-tech startups, as well as between cooperation breadth square and low- and medium-tech startups is significant and negative, indicating that all startups benefit from cooperation breadth, and therefore supporting our Hypothesis 1. However, that coefficient was higher in absolute terms for high-tech startups. To test whether high-tech startups benefit from cooperation breadth to a greater extension than low- and medium-tech startups, we conducted a Wald test. Since it is significant ($\chi^2 = 8.96$, $p < 0.05$), we can conclude that the benefits that get startups when they cooperate are higher in high-tech sectors, confirming our Hypothesis 2.

Finally, we measured cooperation breadth as the ratio of the number of partners' types with to a firm cooperates and the maximum possible number of types of cooperation partners, and then squaring the result to show that an increase at a higher level is seen as larger than an increase at lower levels (Leeuw et al. 2014; Oerlemans et al. 2013). We re-estimated all our models, and the new estimates showed similar results than those found in Table 4 (except for the coefficient of high-tech Startup that turned insignificant), so our hypotheses remain consistent.

Discussion

The aim of this study was to analyse the effect of being a startup and, in particular, being a high-tech startup on the relationship between cooperation breadth and innovation performance. Startups face the liabilities of newness and novelty, and they have not built a resource portfolio yet when they are created (Sirmon et al. 2007), so external sources acquire a crucial role for startups success, being even more important for this type of firms. Our results are in line with previous literature on strategic alliances, which evidenced that startups are more likely to cooperate than incumbent firms (Shan et al. 1994). Startups therefore follow a collaborative entrepreneurial strategy (Burgelman and Hitt 2007), which allow them to overcome their limitations while they explore and exploit business opportunities. The liabilities of smallness and newness are not a limitation for these firms, rather they are a major boost for openness and innovation. In this way, this study extends previous literature since we analyse how startups can benefit from cooperation breadth. Laursen and Salter (2006) analysed the effect of cooperation breadth and depth in firm's innovation performance, and they included startups as control variable, but it was not significant. In this study we deepen in the understanding of openness in startups and their motivation to use external sources. Startups benefit more from knowledge exploration when engage in a diversity of cooperation activities because they need to access to more knowledge and learn from their partners; and they also benefit more from knowledge exploitation when engage in a diversity of cooperation activities because partners offer commercial channels, perform as a sign of quality, bring complementary assets, and share the risks of the innovation processes.

Secondly, we argued that the lack of R&D resources, the inventive capability, the strength to adapt to environmental changes, and the emergence of new markets would make startups to be prone to adopt open innovation strategies in high-tech sectors, and benefit more from cooperation breadth, and we found support for that hypothesis. Although both high-tech and low- and medium-tech firms benefit from cooperation breadth for their innovation performance, those benefits are higher for startups operating in high-tech sectors. Some scholars argued that when other factors, such as firm size, are taken into account, it is not clear openness to be more important in intensive technology sectors (Tether 2002; Chesbrough and Crowther 2006). We analysed the fact of being a startup as a contingency, and we found that high-tech startups benefit from cooperation breadth to a greater extent. Hence, this study complements that literature since the smallness factor might cancel the effect of knowledge-intense sectors, but the newness factor does not.

Conclusion

In conclusion, this study examines how startups and, in particular, high-tech startups may benefit from cooperation breadth on the innovation performance. Startups are forced to open up their boundaries to overcome the liabilities of newness and smallness, and it far from being a limitation, it is an opportunity for triggering knowledge exploration and knowledge exploitation. Cooperation breadth brings more diverse knowledge inputs to identify opportunities and enhances innovation performance, and provide access to market to exploit opportunities, which enhance the innovation performance.

The contributions of this paper are situated at both theoretical and managerial levels. From a theoretical perspective, we contribute to the open innovation literature since it advances in the integration of open innovation with the entrepreneurship literature. Open innovation scholars have underlined the important role of external actors for the startups' innovation processes and have remarked the need for future studies to focus on startups (Bogers et al. 2017; Brunswicker and Van De Vrande 2014; Eftekhari and Bogers 2015). To our best knowledge no previous studies have analysed whether startups benefit to a greater extent from inbound open innovation strategies. The startups' smallness and newness liabilities, rather than being a limitation, they are an incentive for openness. This study also contributes to understand the role of breadth. While previous innovation studies have explained some benefits and disadvantages of breadth, they have not considered its nature. The fact that we find a higher contribution for startups poses that breadth can be used in a different way and it is a tool for innovation. The liabilities of startups make openness to be a necessity to get financial and human resources, and it is a source for startups' knowledge exploration and exploitation. On the one hand, breadth brings diverse knowledge and startups are more dynamic than incumbent firms to integrate heterogeneous knowledge. It leads to the conclusion that the flexibility and dynamism are more important to use external knowledge than having an extensive knowledge base. On the other hand, the fact that startups benefit more from cooperation breadth than other firms means that breadth is a mechanism to access to complementary assets. Since incumbent firms already have a pool of complementary assets, the benefits of openness are bigger for startups. This study further contributes to understand the contingencies on open innovation strategies. We deepen in the relationship between knowledge-intensive industries and openness in startups, and we found that startups in high-tech sectors are the one that benefit the most from cooperation breadth. We contribute to literature through exploring the newness as a contingency factor of the effect of openness in high-tech sectors. While previous literature has argued that the effect of the technology intensity sector tend to disappear when smallness factor is taken into consideration, we explain that the technology intensity sector effect does not disappear when newness factor is taken into consideration. Finally, we contribute to empirical literature since we test our hypotheses on a panel dataset, while most of literature has performed cross-sectional studies.

From a managerial perspective, this study highlights the importance of openness for startups. We found that while cooperation breadth is important for firms, their positive effects are increased if the firm is a startup. Open innovation is a key strategy for startups to outperform their competitors, especially if the startup operates in knowledge-intensive sectors. From a policy perspective, we argue that policy makers should support cooperative programs, making a special emphasis on the relationships between startups and incumbent firms. It would improve the innovation outcomes of a country.

This study has several limitations that can lead to follow-on studies. First, this study has used a panel database to test the hypotheses. The nature of a panel data implies that we have repeated observations on the same cross section of economic agents over time. As a consequence the big sample of startups is introduced when the panel was created or with the two main enlargements (2004, 2005). The startup phenomenon is therefore observed during the first years of the panel, with few observations at the end. Second, we have used random effect Tobit regressions because we observed that the variable innovation performance was left-censored. Other specifications that regard the nature of the data could also be used, for example, an interquartile regression could be applied, so it considers the distribution of the residuals. Third, it would be desirable to use other sampling frames than Spanish firms to extend the validity of the findings. The positive effects that get startups when cooperating with a diversity of partners could be higher in first-runners and technologically-advanced countries, but it could disappear in those based on the imitation of technologies. Fourth, this study has analysed the role of startups as a contingent factor, but other factors, such as the appropriation strategy, could reinforce the differences to openness between high- and low-tech sectors. Lastly, this study also leaves some interesting issues for future research. Our research has focused on the impact of startups on cooperation breadth, but its effect could be dependent on the type of alliance (horizontal, vertical). Future research could analysis whether startups benefit more from cooperating, for example, with universities than with others types of partners. Moreover, startups' benefit could be dependent on the geography of the cooperation. An internationalization perspective would help to understand the knowledge networks spread of a firm and its evolution.

References

Acs, Z. J., Audretsch, D. B., & Lehmann, E. E. (2013). The knowledge spillover theory of entrepreneurship. *Small Business Economics, 41*, 757–774. https://doi.org/10.1007/s11187-013-9505-9.

Alberti, F. G., & Pizzurno, E. (2017). Oops, I did it again! Knowledge leaks in open innovation networks with start-ups. *European Journal of Innovation Management, 20*, 50–79. https://doi.org/10.1108/EJIM-11-2015-0116.

Alkaersig, L., Beukel, K., & Reichstein, T. (2015). *Intellectual property rights management: Rookies, dealers and strategists.* London: Palgrave Macmillan.

Almeida, P., & Kogut, B. (1997). The exploration of technological diversity and geographic localization in innovation: Start-up firms in the semiconductor industry. *Small Business Economics, 9*, 21–31. https://doi.org/10.1023/A:1007995512597.

Almeida, P., Dokko, G., & Rosenkopf, L. (2003). Startup size and the mechanisms of external learning: Increasing opportunity and decreasing ability? *Research Policy, 32*, 301–315. https://doi.org/10.1016/S0048-7333(02)00101-4. Special issue on technology entrepreneurship and contact information for corresponding authors.

Almirall, E., & Casadesus-Masanell, R. (2010). Open versus closed innovation: A model of discovery and divergence. *Academy of Management Review, 35*, 27–47.

Alvarez, S. A., & Barney, J. B. (2001). How entrepreneurial firms can benefit from alliances with large partners. *The Academy of Management Executive (1993–2005), 15*, 139–148.

Audretsch, D. B. (1995). Innovation, growth and survival. *International Journal of Industrial Organization, 13*, 441–457. https://doi.org/10.1016/0167-7187(95)00499-8. The post-entry performance of firms.

Audretsch, D. B., & Lehmann, E. E. (2005). Does the knowledge spillover theory of entrepreneurship hold for regions? *Research Policy, 34*, 1191–1202. https://doi.org/10.1016/j.respol.2005. 03.012. Regionalization of innovation policy.

Audretsch, D. B., Houweling, P., & Thurik, A. R. (2000). Firm survival in the Netherlands. *Review of Industrial Organization, 16*, 1–11. https://doi.org/10.1023/A:1007824501527.

Barge-Gil, A. (2010). Open, semi-open and closed innovators: Towards an explanation of degree of openness. *Industry and Innovation, 17*, 577–607. https://doi.org/10.1080/13662716.2010. 530839.

Bayona, C., Garcıa-Marco, T., & Huerta, E. (2001). Firms' motivations for cooperative R&D: An empirical analysis of Spanish firms. *Research Policy, 30*, 1289–1307. https://doi.org/10.1016/ S0048-7333(00)00151-7.

Belderbos, R., Carree, M., & Lokshin, B. (2004). Cooperative R&D and firm performance. *Research Policy, 33*, 1477–1492. https://doi.org/10.1016/j.respol.2004.07.003.

Bengtsson, L., Lakemond, N., Lazzarotti, V., Manzini, R., Pellegrini, L., & Tell, F. (2015). Open to a select few? Matching partners and knowledge content for open innovation performance. *Creativity and Innovation Management, 24*, 72–86. https://doi.org/10.1111/caim.12098.

Berchicci, L. (2013). Towards an open R&D system: Internal R&D investment, external knowledge acquisition and innovative performance. *Research Policy, 42*, 117–127. https://doi.org/10.1016/ j.respol.2012.04.017.

Bhalla, A., & Terjesen, S. (2013). Cannot make do without you: Outsourcing by knowledge-intensive new firms in supplier networks. *Industrial Marketing Management, 42*, 166–179. https://doi.org/10.1016/j.indmarman.2012.12.005. Managing key supplier relationships.

Blank, S. (2010). *What's a startup? First principles*. Steve Blank.

Bogers, M., Zobel, A.-K., Afuah, A., Almirall, E., Brunswicker, S., Dahlander, L., Frederiksen, L., Gawer, A., Gruber, M., Haefliger, S., Hagedoorn, J., Hilgers, D., Laursen, K., Magnusson, M. G., Majchrzak, A., McCarthy, I. P., Moeslein, K. M., Nambisan, S., Piller, F. T., Radziwon, A., Rossi-Lamastra, C., Sims, J., & Wal, A. L. J. T. (2017). The open innovation research landscape: Established perspectives and emerging themes across different levels of analysis. *Industry and Innovation, 24*, 8–40. https://doi.org/10.1080/13662716.2016.1240068.

Brunswicker, S., & Van De Vrande, V. (2014). Exploring open innovation in small and medium-sized enterprises. In *New frontiers in open innovation*. Oxford: Oxford University Press.

Brunswicker, S., & Vanhaverbeke, W. (2015). Open innovation in small and medium-sized enterprises (SMEs): External knowledge sourcing strategies and internal organizational facilitators. *Journal of Small Business Management, 53*, 1241–1263. https://doi.org/10.1111/jsbm. 12120.

Burgelman, R. A., & Hitt, M. A. (2007). Entrepreneurial actions, innovation, and appropriability. *Strategic Entrepreneurship Journal, 1*, 349–352. https://doi.org/10.1002/sej.28.

Butler, J. E., & Hansen, G. S. (1991). Network evolution, entrepreneurial success, and regional development. *Entrepreneurship and Regional Development, 3*, 1–16. https://doi.org/10.1080/ 08985629100000001.

Cassiman, B., & Veugelers, R. (2002). *Complementarity in the innovation strategy: Internal R&D, external technology acquisition and cooperation* (SSRN scholarly paper no. ID 308601). Rochester, NY: Social Science Research Network.

Cassiman, B., & Veugelers, R. (2006). In search of complementarity in innovation strategy: Internal R&D and external knowledge acquisition. *Management Science, 52*, 68–82. https://doi.org/10. 1287/mnsc.1050.0470.

Chesbrough, H. (2006). Open innovation: A new paradigm for understanding industrial innovation. In H. Chesbrough, W. Vanhaverbeke, & J. West (Eds.), *Open innovation: Researching a new paradigm*. Oxford: Oxford University Press.

Chesbrough, H., & Crowther, A. K. (2006). Beyond high tech: Early adopters of open innovation in other industries. *R&D Management, 36*(3), 229–236. https://doi.org/10.1111/j.1467-9310.2006. 00428.x.

Chesbrough, H. W., & Appleyard, M. M. (2007). Open innovation and strategy. *California Management Review, 50*(1), 57–76. https://doi.org/10.2307/41166416.

Cockburn, I. M., & Henderson, R. M. (1998). Absorptive capacity, coauthoring behavior, and the organization of research in drug discovery. *The Journal of Industrial Economics, 46*, 157–182. https://doi.org/10.1111/1467-6451.00067.

Cohen, W. M., & Levinthal, D. A. (1990). Absorptive capacity: A new perspective on learning and innovation. *Administrative Science Quarterly, 35*, 128–152. https://doi.org/10.2307/2393553.

Coleman, J. S. (1988). Social capital in the creation of human capital. *The American Journal of Sociology, 94*, S95–S120. https://doi.org/10.1086/228943.

Colombelli, A., Krafft, J., & Vivarelli, M. (2016). To be born is not enough: The key role of innovative start-ups. *Small Business Economics*, 1–15. https://doi.org/10.1007/s11187-016-9716-y.

Colombo, M. G., Grilli, L., & Piva, E. (2006). In search of complementary assets: The determinants of alliance formation of high-tech start-ups. *Research Policy, 35*, 1166–1199. https://doi.org/10.1016/j.respol.2006.09.002. Special issue commemorating the 20th anniversary of David Teece's article, "Profiting from Innovation", in Research Policy.

Criscuolo, P., Nicolaou, N., & Salter, A. (2012). The elixir (or burden) of youth? Exploring differences in innovation between start-ups and established firms. *Research Policy, 41*, 319–333. https://doi.org/10.1016/j.respol.2011.12.001.

Dussauge, P., Garrette, B., & Mitchell, W. (2000). Learning from competing partners: Outcomes and durations of scale and link alliances in Europe, North America and Asia. *Strategic Management Journal, 21*, 99–126.

Dyer, J. H., & Singh, H. (1998). The relational view: Cooperative strategy and sources of interorganizational competitive advantage. *Academy of Management Review, 23*, 660–679. https://doi.org/10.5465/AMR.1998.1255632.

Eftekhari, N., & Bogers, M. (2015). Open for entrepreneurship: How open innovation can foster new venture creation. *Creativity and Innovation Management, 24*, 574–584. https://doi.org/10.1111/caim.12136.

Eisenhardt, K. M., & Schoonhoven, C. B. (1996). Resource-based view of strategic alliance formation: Strategic and social effects in entrepreneurial firms. *Organization Science, 7*, 136–150.

Escribano, A., Fosfuri, A., & Tribó, J. A. (2009). Managing external knowledge flows: The moderating role of absorptive capacity. *Research Policy, 38*, 96–105. https://doi.org/10.1016/j.respol.2008.10.022.

Etemad, H., & Wright, R. W. (1999). Internationalization of SMEs: Management responses to a changing environment. *Journal of International Marketing, 7*, 4–10.

Faems, D., Van Looy, B., & Debackere, K. (2005). Interorganizational collaboration and innovation: Toward a portfolio approach. *Journal of Product Innovation Management, 22*, 238–250. https://doi.org/10.1111/j.0737-6782.2005.00120.x.

Faems, D., De Visser, M., Andries, P., & Van Looy, B. (2010). Technology alliance portfolios and financial performance: Value-enhancing and cost-increasing effects of open innovation. *Journal of Product Innovation Management, 27*, 785–796. https://doi.org/10.1111/j.1540-5885.2010.00752.x.

Gans, J. S., & Stern, S. (2003). The product market and the market for 'ideas': Commercialization strategies for technology entrepreneurs. *Research Policy, 32*, 333–350. https://doi.org/10.1016/S0048-7333(02)00103-8. Special issue on technology entrepreneurship and contact information for corresponding authors.

Gassmann, O. (2006). Opening up the innovation process: Towards an agenda. *R&D Management, 36*, 223–228. https://doi.org/10.1111/j.1467-9310.2006.00437.x.

Gassmann, O., Enkel, E., & Chesbrough, H. (2010). The future of open innovation. *R&D Management, 40*, 213–221. https://doi.org/10.1111/j.1467-9310.2010.00605.x.

Gimenez-Fernandez, E. M., & Beukel, K. (2017). Open innovation and the comparison between startups and incumbent firms in Spain. *Universia Business Review, 0*, 18–33. https://doi.org/10.3232/UBR.2017.V14.N3.01.

Gimenez-Fernandez, E. M., & Sandulli, F. D. (2016). Modes of inbound knowledge flows: Are cooperation and outsourcing really complementary? *Industry and Innovation, 0*, 1–22. https://doi.org/10.1080/13662716.2016.1266928.

Grant, R. M., & Baden-Fuller, C. (2004). A knowledge accessing theory of strategic alliances. *Journal of Management Studies, 41*, 61–84. https://doi.org/10.1111/j.1467-6486.2004.00421.x.

Grimpe, C., & Kaiser, U. (2010). Balancing internal and external knowledge acquisition: The gains and pains from R&D outsourcing. *Journal of Management Studies, 47*, 1483–1509. https://doi.org/10.1111/j.1467-6486.2010.00946.x.

Gruber, M., Heinemann, F., Brettel, M., & Hungeling, S. (2010). Configurations of resources and capabilities and their performance implications: An exploratory study on technology ventures. *Strategic Management Journal, 31*, 1337–1356. https://doi.org/10.1002/smj.865.

Gruber, M., MacMillan, I. C., & Thompson, J. D. (2013). Escaping the prior knowledge corridor: What shapes the number and variety of market opportunities identified before market entry of technology start-ups? *Organization Science, 24*, 280–300. https://doi.org/10.1287/orsc.1110.0721.

Gulati, R., Nohria, N., & Zaheer, A. (2000). Strategic networks. *Strategic Management Journal, 21*, 203–215. https://doi.org/10.1002/(SICI)1097-0266(200003)21:3<203::AID-SMJ102>3.0.CO;2-K.

Haans, R. F. J., Pieters, C., & He, Z.-L. (2016). Thinking about U: Theorizing and testing U- and inverted U-shaped relationships in strategy research. *Strategic Management Journal, 37*, 1177–1195. https://doi.org/10.1002/smj.2399.

Haeussler, C., Patzelt, H., & Zahra, S. A. (2012). Strategic alliances and product development in high technology new firms: The moderating effect of technological capabilities. *Journal of Business Venturing, 27*, 217–233. https://doi.org/10.1016/j.jbusvent.2010.10.002.

Hayter, C. S. (2013). Conceptualizing knowledge-based entrepreneurship networks: Perspectives from the literature. *Small Business Economics, 41*, 899–911. https://doi.org/10.1007/s11187-013-9512-x.

Hite, J. M., & Hesterly, W. S. (2001). The evolution of firm networks: From emergence to early growth of the firm. *Strategic Management Journal, 22*, 275–286. https://doi.org/10.1002/smj.156.

Hoang, H., & Antoncic, B. (2003). Network-based research in entrepreneurship: A critical review. *Journal of Business Venturing, 18*, 165–187. https://doi.org/10.1016/S0883-9026(02)00081-2.

Huizingh, E. K. R. E. (2010). Open innovation: State of the art and future perspectives. *Technovation, 31*, 2–9. https://doi.org/10.1016/j.technovation.2010.10.002.

Hyytinen, A., Pajarinen, M., & Rouvinen, P. (2015). Does innovativeness reduce startup survival rates? *Journal of Business Venturing, 30*(4), 564–581. https://doi.org/10.1016/j.jbusvent.2014.10.001.

Katila, R., & Ahuja, G. (2002). Something old, something new: A longitudinal study of search behavior and new product introduction. *Academy of Management Journal, 45*, 1183–1194. https://doi.org/10.2307/3069433.

Katila, R., & Shane, S. (2005). When does lack of resources make new firms innovative? *Academy of Management Journal, 48*, 814–829. https://doi.org/10.5465/AMJ.2005.18803924.

Larson, A., & Starr, J. A. (1993). A network model of organization formation. *Entrepreneurship Theory and Practice, 17*, 5–16.

Laursen, K., & Salter, A. (2006). Open for innovation: The role of openness in explaining innovation performance among U.K. manufacturing firms. *Strategic Management Journal, 27*, 131–150. https://doi.org/10.1002/smj.507.

Laursen, K., & Salter, A. J. (2014). The paradox of openness: Appropriability, external search and collaboration. *Research Policy, 43*, 867–878. https://doi.org/10.1016/j.respol.2013.10.004. Open innovation: New insights and evidence.

Lechner, C., & Dowling, M. (2003). Firm networks: External relationships as sources for the growth and competitiveness of entrepreneurial firms. *Entrepreneurship and Regional Development, 15*, 1–26. https://doi.org/10.1080/08985620210159220.

Lee, H., Kelley, D., Lee, J., & Lee, S. (2012). SME survival: The impact of internationalization, technology resources, and alliances. *Journal of Small Business Management, 50*, 1–19. https://doi.org/10.1111/j.1540-627X.2011.00341.x.

Leeuw, T., Lokshin, B., & Duysters, G. (2014). Returns to alliance portfolio diversity: The relative effects of partner diversity on firm's innovative performance and productivity. *Journal of Business Research, 67*, 1839–1849. https://doi.org/10.1016/j.jbusres.2013.12.005.

Leiponen, A., & Helfat, C. E. (2010). Innovation objectives, knowledge sources, and the benefits of breadth. *Strategic Management Journal, 31,* 224–236. https://doi.org/10.1002/smj.807.

Levitt, B., & March, J. G. (1988). Organizational learning. *Annual Review of Sociology, 14,* 319–338. https://doi.org/10.1146/annurev.so.14.080188.001535.

Lin, B.-W. (2003). Technology transfer as technological learning: A source of competitive advantage for firms with limited R&D resources. *R&D Management, 33,* 327–341. https://doi.org/10.1111/1467-9310.00301.

Lin, E. S., Hsiao, Y.-C., & Lin, H. (2013). Complementarities of R&D strategies on innovation performance: Evidence from Taiwanese manufacturing firms. *Technological and Economic Development of Economy, 19,* S134–S156. https://doi.org/10.3846/20294913.2013.876684.

Luker, W., & Lyons, D. (1997). Employment shifts in high-technology industries, 1988-96. *Monthly Labor Review, 120,* 12–25.

March, J. G. (1991). Exploration and exploitation in organizational learning. *Organization Science, 2,* 71–87. https://doi.org/10.1287/orsc.2.1.71.

Martinez, M. A., & Aldrich, H. E. (2011). Networking strategies for entrepreneurs: Balancing cohesion and diversity. *International Journal of Entrepreneurial Behavior and Research, 17,* 7–38. https://doi.org/10.1108/13552551111107499.

Michelino, F., Cammarano, A., Lamberti, E., & Caputo, M. (2017). Open innovation for start-ups: A patent-based analysis of bio-pharmaceutical firms at the knowledge domain level. *European Journal of Innovation Management, 20,* 112–134. https://doi.org/10.1108/EJIM-10-2015-0103.

Nelson, R. R., & Winter, S. G. (1982). The Schumpeterian tradeoff revisited. *The American Economic Review, 72,* 114–132.

Neyens, I., Faems, D., & Sels, L. (2010). The impact of continuous and discontinuous alliance strategies on startup innovation performance. *International Journal of Technology Management, 52,* 392–410. https://doi.org/10.1504/IJTM.2010.035982.

Nieto, M. J., & Santamaría, L. (2007). The importance of diverse collaborative networks for the novelty of product innovation. *Technovation, 27,* 367–377. https://doi.org/10.1016/j.technovation.2006.10.001.

OECD. (2005). *Oslo manual: Guidelines for collecting and interpreting innovation data* (3rd ed.). Paris: Organisation for Economic Co-operation and Development.

Oerlemans, L. A. G., Knoben, J., & Pretorius, M. W. (2013). Alliance portfolio diversity, radical and incremental innovation: The moderating role of technology management. *Technovation, 33,* 234–246. https://doi.org/10.1016/j.technovation.2013.02.004.

Pangarkar, N., & Wu, J. (2013). Alliance formation, partner diversity, and performance of Singapore startups. *Asia Pacific Journal of Management, 30,* 791–807. https://doi.org/10.1007/s10490-012-9305-9.

Parida, V., Westerberg, M., & Frishammar, J. (2012). Inbound open innovation activities in high-tech SMEs: The impact on innovation performance. *Journal of Small Business Management, 50,* 283–309. https://doi.org/10.1111/j.1540-627X.2012.00354.x.

Pisano, G. (2006). Profiting from innovation and the intellectual property revolution. *Research Policy, 35,* 1122–1130. https://doi.org/10.1016/j.respol.2006.09.008. Special issue commemorating the 20th anniversary of David Teece's article, "Profiting from Innovation", in Research Policy.

Rohrbeck, R. (2010). Harnessing a network of experts for competitive advantage: Technology scouting in the ICT industry. *R&D Management, 40,* 169–180. https://doi.org/10.1111/j.1467-9310.2010.00601.x.

Santamaría, L., Nieto, M. J., & Barge-Gil, A. (2009). Beyond formal R&D: Taking advantage of other sources of innovation in low- and medium-technology industries. *Research Policy, 38,* 507–517. https://doi.org/10.1016/j.respol.2008.10.004.

Sapienza, H. J., Autio, E., George, G., & Zahra, S. A. (2006). A capabilities perspective on the effects of early internationalization on firm survival and growth. *Academy of Management Review, 31,* 914–933. https://doi.org/10.5465/AMR.2006.22527465.

Schmiedeberg, C. (2008). Complementarities of innovation activities: An empirical analysis of the German manufacturing sector. *Research Policy, 37*, 1492–1503. https://doi.org/10.1016/j.respol.2008.07.008.

Schroll, A., & Mild, A. (2011). Open innovation modes and the role of internal R&D. *European Journal of Innovation Management, 14*, 475–495. https://doi.org/http://0-dx.doi.org.cisne.sim.ucm.es/10.1108/14601061111174925.

Schumpeter, J. A. (1934). *The theory of economic development: An inquiry into profits, capital, credit, interest, and the business cycle*. New Brunswick, NJ: Transaction Publishers.

Segers, J.-P. (2015). The interplay between new technology based firms, strategic alliances and open innovation, within a regional systems of innovation context. The case of the biotechnology cluster in Belgium. *Journal of Global Entrepreneurship Research, 5*, 1–17. https://doi.org/10.1186/s40497-015-0034-7.

Shan, W., Walker, G., & Kogut, B. (1994). Interfirm cooperation and startup innovation in the biotechnology industry. *Strategic Management Journal, 15*, 387–394. https://doi.org/10.1002/smj.4250150505.

Sirmon, D. G., Hitt, M. A., & Ireland, R. D. (2007). Managing firm resources in dynamic environments to create value: Looking inside the black box. *Academy of Management Review, 32*, 273–292. https://doi.org/10.5465/AMR.2007.23466005.

Spender, J.-C. (1992). Limits to learning from the west: How western management advice may prove limited in Eastern Europe. *International Executive, 34*, 389–413. https://doi.org/10.1002/tie.5060340503.

Spender, J.-C., Corvello, V., Grimaldi, M., & Rippa, P. (2017). Startups and open innovation: A review of the literature. *European Journal of Innovation Management, 20*, 4–30. https://doi.org/10.1108/EJIM-12-2015-0131.

Spithoven, A., Clarysse, B., & Knockaert, M. (2011). Building absorptive capacity to organise inbound open innovation in traditional industries. *Technovation, 31*, 10–21. https://doi.org/10.1016/j.technovation.2010.10.003.

Spithoven, A., Vanhaverbeke, W., & Roijakkers, N. (2013). Open innovation practices in SMEs and large enterprises. *Small Business Economics, 41*, 537–562. https://doi.org/10.1007/s11187-012-9453-9.

Stinchcombe, A. L. (1965). Organizations and social structure. *Handbook of Organizations, 44*, 142–193.

Teece, D. J. (1986). Profiting from technological innovation: Implications for integration, collaboration, licensing and public policy. *Research Policy, 15*, 285–305. https://doi.org/10.1016/0048-7333(86)90027-2.

Tether, B. S. (2002). Who co-operates for innovation, and why: An empirical analysis. *Research Policy, 31*, 947–967. https://doi.org/10.1016/S0048-7333(01)00172-X.

Tobin, J. (1958). Estimation of relationships for limited dependent variables. *Econometrica, 26*, 24–36. https://doi.org/10.2307/1907382.

Toh, P. K., & Kim, T. (2013). Why put all your eggs in one basket? A competition-based view of how technological uncertainty affects a firm's technological specialization. *Organization Science, 24*, 1214–1236. https://doi.org/10.1287/orsc.1120.0782.

Un, C. A., Cuervo-Cazurra, A., & Asakawa, K. (2010). R&D collaborations and product innovation. *Journal of Product Innovation Management, 27*, 673–689. https://doi.org/10.1111/j.1540-5885.2010.00744.x.

Usman, M., & Vanhaverbeke, W. (2017). How start-ups successfully organize and manage open innovation with large companies. *European Journal of Innovation Management, 20*, 171–186. https://doi.org/10.1108/EJIM-07-2016-0066.

Van de Vrande, V. (2013). Balancing your technology-sourcing portfolio: How sourcing mode diversity enhances innovative performance. *Strategic Management Journal, 34*, 610–621. https://doi.org/10.1002/smj.2031.

von Tunzelmann, N., & Acha, V. (2006). Innovation in "Low-Tech" industries. https://doi.org/10.1093/oxfordhb/9780199286805.003.0015.

Wadhwa, A., & Kotha, S. (2006). Knowledge creation through external venturing: Evidence from the telecommunications equipment manufacturing industry. *Academy of Management Journal, 49*, 819–835. https://doi.org/10.5465/AMJ.2006.22083132.

Walker, G., Kogut, B., & Shan, W. (1997). Social capital, structural holes and the formation of an industry network. *Organization Science, 8*, 109–125. https://doi.org/10.1287/orsc.8.2.109.

Wang, H., Wuebker, R. J., Han, S., & Ensley, M. D. (2012). Strategic alliances by venture capital backed firms: An empirical examination. *Small Business Economics, 38*, 179–196. https://doi.org/http://0-dx.doi.org.cisne.sim.ucm.es/10.1007/s11187-009-9247-x.

Wang, Y., Roijakkers, N., & Vanhaverbeke, W. (2013). Learning-by-licensing: How Chinese firms benefit from licensing-in technologies. *IEEE Transactions on Engineering Management, 60*, 46–58. https://doi.org/10.1109/TEM.2012.2205578.

Yu, J., Gilbert, B. A., & Oviatt, B. M. (2011). Effects of alliances, time, and network cohesion on the initiation of foreign sales by new ventures. *Strategic Management Journal, 32*, 424–446. https://doi.org/10.1002/smj.884.

Zobel, A.-K. (2013). *Open innovation: A dynamic capabilities perspective*. Maastricht: Maastricht University.

Elena M. Gimenez-Fernandez is Professor of Operations Management at Rey Juan Carlos University (Spain). She has been a visiting student at the University of California, Berkeley, and at the University of Copenhagen. Her main interests center on open innovation and entrepreneurship. She graduated with cum laude for her PhD in Business at Complutense University in Madrid (Spain), and she was awarded with a National Prize for her degree in business. She has received honors for her research that include Finalist for the XV Young Award in the category of economy from Complutense Foundation.

Marcel Bogers is a Full Professor of Innovation and Entrepreneurship at Department of Food and Resource Economics, the Unit for Innovation, Entrepreneurship and Management, University of Copenhagen. He is a Garwood Research Fellow at the Haas School of Business at the University of California, Berkeley. He obtained a PhD in Management of Technology from Ecole Polytechnique Fédérale de Lausanne (Swiss Federal Institute of Technology). His main interests center on openness and participation in innovation and entrepreneurial processes, with particular topics being business models, open innovation, users as innovators, collaborative prototyping, family firms, improvisation, and university–industry collaboration.

Francesco Sandulli is a UCM-Orange Chair, Complutense University of Madrid, Spain. Achievements include research in brand identity web analysis method and research in information technology productivity. He is recipient of Best Thesis on Management award, Complutense University, 2003, and Young Economist award, Fundacion Complutense, 2004.

Open Innovation Models for Increased Innovation Activities and Enterprise Growth

Gadaf Rexhepi, Hyrije Abazi, Amir Rahdari, and Biljana Angelova

Abstract Open innovation tends to be one of the hottest topic in innovation management. Open innovation tends to be very much related with enterprise growth. The purpose of this paper is to present a literature review related to open innovation and open innovation models and how they affect enterprise growth. The book chapter represents the importance of innovation and open innovation overall and open innovation. Special emphasize in this paper is given to the evolution of open innovation models and how this has influence enterprise effectiveness and efficiency which further influence enterprise growth.

Introduction

Innovation has become the new buzzword across the globe. Most of the international organizations, governments, corporate, academia and civil society accept innovation as the answer to major contemporary challenges (Carayannis and Campbell 2011; Rexhepi et al. 2017). Organizations in today's economy tend to change and adopt continuously (Rexhepi and Berisha 2017). Some of these changes are political transformation such as the rise of a multipolar world and loss of sovereignty of nation states; technological revolutions in informatics and biotechnology; and one of very important elements global environmental change (Carayannis and Campbell 2011).

Innovations and alternatives are emerging, not only in businesses in industrialized countries but also in developing countries (China in solar technology, and mobile banking in Kenya) (Carayannis and Campbell 2011). Innovation needs to focus on the integration of fundamental and applied research; it makes shifts in mindsets,

G. Rexhepi (✉) · H. Abazi
South-East European University, Tetovo, Macedonia
e-mail: g.rexhepi@seeu.edu.mk

A. Rahdari
Tarbiat Modares University, Tehran, Iran

B. Angelova
University St "Cyril and Methodius", Skopje, Macedonia

© Springer Nature Switzerland AG 2019   37
G. Rexhepi et al. (eds.), *Open Innovation and Entrepreneurship*,
https://doi.org/10.1007/978-3-030-16912-1_3

strategy, research focus, academia-industry relationships, IP policies and government involvement (Parveen et al. 2015).

However, the main change regarding innovation is the source of innovations. Innovations usually are seen as a product that derives from inside the organizations and produce competitive advantage also known as *closed innovation*. Nevertheless, research have proven that this way of exploring innovation have many boundaries, even though researchers have identified a number of ways in which business strategies can influence innovation activities (Kennedy et al. 2016; Rexhepi 2015). Thus, they recommend new sources of innovation, which will come from outside the organization known as *open innovation.* The new approach toward the source of innovation for organizations every day is increasing. Parveen et al. (2015), argued that there are some antecedents that helped play a key role in both enabling the ideas of open innovation and its acceptance among managers and scholars. *First, innovation scholars have understood since the 1970s that sources of innovative ideas often come from outside the firm. Second, open innovation builds on the profiting from innovation framework, paying specific attention to challenges that firms face capturing returns from their innovative effort. This tradition is rooted in an understanding of the particular features of technology markets, with asymmetric relations between bargaining agents, and incomplete information and contracts* (Arora et al. 2001; Gans and Stern 2003; Parveen et al. 2015).

According the EU's Open Innovation Strategy and Policy Group (OISPG) yearbooks about the current innovation practices in Europe there is an increase of level of open-ness with increased sophistication and complexity associated with innovation (Curley and Salmelin 2013). However, in many cases firms hesitate to open their innovation processes or are not able to build the necessary capabilities (de Araújo Burcharth et al. 2014), neither for successful innovation alliances and partnerships nor for the integration of their customer's creativity (Arora and Gambardella 1990; Bruneel et al. 2010).

The models of open innovation, which will be explain in this chapter, contribute to sustainability of enterprises. A study done by Rauter et al. (2017), found that by qualitatively analyzing 19 papers that were published between 2003 and 2015 showed that open innovation is an important concept for sustainability (Rauter et al. 2017). The intersection of mega-trends such as digitization, mass collaboration, and sustainability needs are creating unique opportunities which results in increase shared value because of innovation (Curley and Salmelin 2013). Sustainability oriented firms tend to increase their attention to how firms may improve environmental and/or social performance and in this way trying to increase its competitiveness (Kennedy et al. 2016). Open innovation can be used for sustainable development especially in a low-tech environment, mainly because in low-tech environments open innovation emergesgradually from the spillovers of R&D (Ingenbleek and Backus 2015).

In this chapter firstly we discuss about innovation, role of open innovation in sustainability, we explain the concept of open innovation and explain the models of open innovation and how they emerge.

Open Innovation

In technology-intensive industries, innovation is a central issue for the competitiveness of the firm (Ferrary 2011). This is why most successful companies invest huge amounts of their resources in R&D (for example, in 2008, Microsoft invested $6.4 billion in R&D; Nokia, 5.3 billion; IBM, $4.3 billion; Intel, $4.1 billion and Motorola, $2.9 billion) (Ferrary 2011). However, new global challenges require new smarter solutions such as healthcare, transportation, climate change, youth unemployment, financial stability, prosperity, sustainability, and growth which can be a great opportunity in generating new shared value (Curley and Salmelin 2013; Suklev and Rexhepi 2013). As Joseph Schumpeter's (1942) in his famous creative destruction model stated that, where the failure of old approaches fuels the motivation for change will appear (Curley and Salmelin 2013). Open innovation showed to be the new model that can help reshape the way organizations use innovation capacity.

Institutional openness is becoming increasingly popular in practice and academia: open innovation, open R&D and open business models (Gassmann et al. 2010). Organization is an open system, it influences and, can be influenced from the society. This means that organizations create benefits for others but also can use benefits from other. Creativity and innovation is the first thing that organization should cooperate with others. The new concept introduced by Henry Chesbrough (2003), called open Innovation conceptualized the idea of innovation where ideas pass to and from different organizations for exploitation. Open innovation concept assumes that corporate innovation activities are more like an open system than the traditional (twentieth century) vertically integrated model (Chesbrough 2003, 2006). Open innovation concepts suggest that innovation can be derive not just from inside the organization but also from outside the organization. Chesbrough et al. (2011), suggest companies should find a way to utilize the distributed pools of knowledge possessed by customers, suppliers, universities, national labs, consortia, consultants and even their own competitors. The combination of diverse knowledge increases the chances of finding creative solutions leading to innovations that are more radical.

The open innovation concept has been developed firstly from a small club of innovation practitioners, mostly active in high-tech industries, to a widely discussed and implemented innovation practice (Gassmann et al. 2010). Today, open innovation is cited in strategy, general management and organization behavior journals (Gassmann et al. 2010). The concept of open innovation has, penetrated in industries such as software, electronics, telecommunications, pharma and biotech, while the software and electronics industries are progressively building on the open innovation trend (Chesbrough 2003). Organizations such as SAP and Microsoft have started to build decentralized research labs on university campuses to increase their absorptive capacity for outside-in innovation processes, Apple, had to open up its proprietary technology to its addicted high-tech users, Philips open innovation park, Xerox's Palo Alto Research Center, Siemens' open innovation program and IBM's open source initiatives, British Telecom's incubation activities, Deutsche Telecom and

Swisscom all of them drive open innovation on a strategic level (Gassmann et al. 2010). It is obvious that the era of open innovation has just begun (Gassmann et al. 2010).

Open innovation has been defined as *'... the use of purposive inflows and outflows of knowledge to accelerate internal innovation, and expand the markets for external use of innovation, respectively'* (Chesbrough et al. 2006). Nevertheless, open innovation definition has evolved through year, even Chesbrough's definition of open innovation (Parveen et al. 2015). Open innovation is seen also as a *"distributed innovation process based on purposively managed knowledge flows across organizational boundaries, using pecuniary and non-pecuniary mechanisms in line with the organization's business model"* (Chesbrough and Bogers 2014). Open innovation is also seen as *a methodology to design and implement solutions collaboratively by engaging all stakeholders in an iterative and inclusive service design process* (Carayannis and Campbell 2011). It is used to address issues for businesses, governments and many other institutions in order to improve the quality of their innovation activities and increase quality of their service that they deliver (Syla and Rexhepi 2013).

The use of open innovation is diverse among countries. In countries such as Chile, Colombia, Egypt, and Lebanon open innovation activities are oriented to develop tangible and actionable opportunities for government practitioners to work together with citizens to tackle intractable challenges in issues ranging from urban and governance to mobility and water. In addition, in other countries like in Finland, the Republic of Korea, Spain use open innovation in cities to support entrepreneurship and build creative confidence among diverse stakeholders as governments and academia (Carayannis and Campbell 2011). Companies that create innovation using open innovation concept use different approach toward innovation also, meaning if one innovation can't be used for personal use this can be sold to other companies that might have the right model and this innovation might work (Vanhaverbeke et al. 2008).

Open innovation in risk-laden processes that includes some advantages. *First, firms can benefit from early involvement in new technologies or business opportunities. Second, firms can profit from delayed financial commitment as they can invest step-by-step, avoiding investing large up-front costs. Third, they can benefit from early exits, as corporate venturing is a flexible investment instrument. Fourth, investing firms can also delay exit in the case of spins-offs* (Vanhaverbeke et al. 2008).

Gassmann et al. (2010) suggest nine perspectives needed to develop an open innovation theory more fully. Open innovation is based on these different research streams, which are:

1. The *spatial perspective*
2. The *structural perspective*
3. The *user perspective.*
4. The *supplier perspective.*
5. The *leveraging perspective.*

6. The *process perspective.*
7. The *tool perspective.*
8. The *institutional perspective.*
9. The *cultural perspective.*

The number of streams is not definitive, new may arise. However, even though the concept of open innovation has evolved still it is commonly associated with fast-growing, technology-intensive industries (Sarkar and Costa 2008).

Open Innovation Models

The literature on the dynamics of the development of innovation system framework has undergone through different phases. There is a vast empirical evidence on open innovation itself, albeit few of them consider the innovation system framework approach. The primary model of knowledge production, Triple Helix, developed by Etzkowitz and Leydesdorff (2000), represented innovation system model through the interactions of three 'helices' in knowledge production: academia/universities (higher education), industry (economy), and governments. One of the advantages of using the Triple Helix model in qualitative research is related with the increased awareness about knowledge-based developments needs *at least* three relevant dimensions (Leydesdorff 2012). Triple Helix model motivates scholars to reflect on more than two possible dynamics (markets and governance) (Leydesdorff 2012).

Studies have shown that increased cooperation and knowledge transfer from Universities to the other business institutions offer opportunities for increased regional innovation and commercialization possibilities (Miller et al. 2016). Knowledge transfer within the Triple Helix is conceptualized as boundary spanning across academia, Industry and regional Government (Miller et al. 2016). The model of "Open Innovations" (OI) can be compared with the "Triple Helix of University-Industry-Government Relations" (TH) as attempts to find surplus value in bringing industrial innovation closer to public R&D (Leydesdorff and Ivanova 2016).

Etzkowitz and Leydesdorff (2000), not only consider the "university-industry-government relations" and networks, but further highlighting the overlap of the three helices on "tri-lateral networks and hybrid organizations". Accordingly, at this stage of the model of knowledge production, the so far individual entities have joint their strength, thus resulting into the synergy of the interaction itself between academia, industry and the state (Etzkowitz and Leydesdorff 2000). Having said that this is the primary model of knowledge production, as such it is regarded as useful innovation framework where the interaction between universities, the whole economy and the institutions of government develops through intense, but nonlinear, communication and negotiations (Etzkowitz and Leydesdorff 2000; Leydesdorff and Etzkowitz 1996).

Gibbons et al. developed a theory of the knowledge production of Mode 1 and Mode 2, which are also being used to further explain the concept of the Triple Helix. Mode 1 of this theory refers to the production of scientific knowledge in a traditional university setting, whereas Mode 2 is established as a supplement to Mode 1. According to them, in Mode 2 science has gone 'beyond the market!' where knowledge production becomes diffused throughout society. In this early study, Mode 2 is characterized by the following principles: 'knowledge produced in the context of application'; 'transdisciplinarity'; 'heterogeneity and organizational diversity'; 'social accountability and reflexivity'; and 'quality control'. Consequently, the boundaries between science and technology start to fade, as the university-based scientific research is spread in a larger societal context, i.e. bridging universities with business and linking science and technology closer together became necessary (Campbell and Güttel 2005).

Further investigation in this field of research has come up with the concept of *academic firm*. According to Campbell et al. (2013), academic firm represents a type of firm that focuses on encouraging, supporting, and advancing knowledge production and knowledge application. Taking into consideration that this type of firm follows the logic of a "sustainability" in balance with knowledge production and the principles of knowledge production, even though the academic firm is also inclined to generate profit (revenues), it is contrary to the concept of the "commercial firm".

Companies and universities usually are not able to capture the full potential from their cooperation. The term 'open innovation' was firstly used by Henry Chesbrough to describe, "how useful knowledge and technology was becoming increasingly widespread," and how we can benefit from integrating knowledge and expertise in the economics of innovation (Melese et al. 2009). There are also studies that question the capacities of separate entities. For example, Alexander et al., analyze the university capacity, thus question their ability to become truly open and at the same time provide academic faculty that will be engaged in collaboration and impact. This study emphasizes the fact that together with the development of the innovation system universities are challenged to rethink their models of engagement with industry and wider society.

Pharmaceutical and large biotechnology companies, even though they increased their spending on research and development (R&D) by 147% from 1993 to 2004 to fuel their drug pipelines, still they achieved to do so by just 38%. Thus, many companies realized that they needed to look beyond their own walls for innovation (Melese et al. 2009).

But in order for this cooperation university-industry, there are several steps to take in consideration (Melese et al. 2009):

(i) recognize the value proposition of the collaboration;
(ii) manage the industry-academic collaborations as they would an investment portfolio;
(iii) adopt a new attitude about sharing of information; and
(iv) create new innovative models. An approach to each of these steps is detailed below.

Firms need to continuously look for new growth opportunities (Vanhaverbeke et al. 2008). The investigation in the field noticed that Triple Helix model has its disadvantages, as it does not take into consideration the *civil society*.

In continuation of 'Mode 1' and 'Mode 2', Carayannis and Campbell (2009), introduce the 'Mode 3' system consisting of 'Innovation Networks' and 'Knowledge Clusters'. *"This is a multi-layered, multi-modal, multi-nodal and multi-lateral system, encompassing mutually complementary and reinforcing innovation networks and knowledge clusters consisting of human and intellectual capital, shaped by social capital and underpinned by financial capital."* The basic idea of the Carayannis and Campbell (2009), is: co-existence, co-evolution and co-specialisation of different knowledge paradigms and different knowledge modes of knowledge production and knowledge use as well as their co-specialisation as a result.

Another related approach is the one with helices. In extension of the Triple Helix model, Carayannis and Campbell (2009) suggest a 'Quadruple Helix Innovation System Framework', which in addition to the above stated helices, has a 'fourth helix' identified as the 'media-based and culture-based public'. In other words, the new framework of the innovation model is transformed to the Quadruple Helix, which is embedding the features of the public to the Triple Helix (Carayannis and Campbell 2009). The quadruple helix model of innovation involves civil society with business, academia, and government sectors with aim to drive changes (Curley and Salmelin 2013).

The *innovation users* are another element emphasized by Carayannis et al. (2017), on the Quadruple Helix Innovation System Framework. The role that the civil society have (i.e. users), are at the heart of innovations and encourage their development. In other words, they are the owners and drivers of the innovation processes. Considering the involvement of users in their role as lead users, co-developers, and co-creators, Arnkil et al. (2010), maintain that the degree of user involvement could be defined as inclusive of the 'design by users' to develop new innovative products, services and solutions. Accordingly, civil society as the fourth helix has become a crucial helix of innovation systems, and the model itself considers the innovation economy with four, all equally important, helices: universities, firms, government and civil society.

Leydesdorff (2012), argue that in the case of Japan, the addition of a fourth helix to the model was needed because along with university–industry–government relations, internationalization had also an impact during the 1990s, mainly because of the new economic approaches of China and the demise of the Soviet Union. Based on qualitative empirical research, MacGregor et al. present and analyze the current innovation architecture to support cooperation, co-specialization, and coopetition between actors, and the main functions carried out within the system, while exploring the readiness for the quadruple helix in 16 European innovation ecosystems, all within medium-sized cities. They discuss whether quadruple-helix innovation architecture (Q-HIA) evolves from triple-helix architectures.

To determine whether the Quadruple Helix model has an effect on the firms' profitability, Campanella et al. (2017) employed the classification analysis method (Classification and Regression Trees) on a sample of 4215 manufacturing firms located in science parks. In order to deal with the variable "citizen" they classify it as businesses with high Return on Investment. Their findings show that in science parks "the fourth helix" (citizen) has an important role in classifying the firms with the highest performance. Moreover, the majority of firms that attribute high importance to the collaboration with private financial institutions in order to finance innovations have a high ROI. In addition, firms with high economic performance in the model of the quadruple helix generate product innovation.

Campbell et al. (2013) consider the perspective of knowledge democracy through Quadruple Helix. They emphasize that the architectures of Quadruple Helix (and Quintuple Helix) innovation systems demand and require the formation of a democracy, implicating that quality of democracy provides for a support and encouragement of innovation and innovation systems, so that quality of democracy and progress of innovation mutually "Cross-Helix" in a connecting and amplifying mode and manner (Campbell et al. 2013).

The use of Quadruple Helix Innovation Theory (QHIT) proved that the investment in innovation transmission mechanisms influence the economic growth and productivity gains (Afonso et al. 2010). Quadruple helix model for open innovation argues the integration of industry, academia, government and society is inevitable for the organizations development. This caused challenges to the organizations to respond dynamic environment (Parveen et al. 2015).

Quadruple Helix reflects in many ways several features, which are related to new thinking in innovation process and innovation policy (Parveen et al. 2015). Study investigated the impact of organization culture on quadruple helix and it was found that to optimize the open innovation in context of industry, academia, society and government organization are required to be committed to the open innovation implementation (Parveen et al. 2015). As discussed earlier in this chapter, the Triple Helix innovation model is concentrated on university-industry-government relations, whereas the Quadruple Helix embeds the Triple Helix by adding as a fourth helix the 'media-based and culture-based public' and 'civil society'. The latest development considers the Quintuple Helix innovation model which includes the helix (and perspective) of the 'natural environments of society' (Carayannis et al. 2012). The more recent research on innovation system framework has come up with the fifth helix. Figure 1 represents a Quintuple Helix Innovation System Framework.

The Quintuple Helix innovation model, presented by Carayannis et al. (2012), is even broader and more comprehensive by contextualizing the Quadruple Helix and by additionally adding the helix (and perspective) of the *natural environments of*

Fig. 1 Five elements of the Quintuple Helix

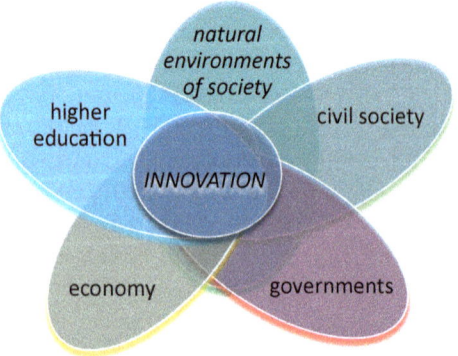

society'. The Quintuple Helix helps all parties win like ecology, knowledge and innovation, or creating synergies between economy, society, and democracy and even global warning (Carayannis et al. 2012).

All systems in a *Quintuple Helix* perform a pivotal function, influencing each other (Carayannis et al. 2012). The *Quintuple Helix Model* shows that an investment in knowledge and promoting it influences new and crucial impulses for innovation, know-how and overall advancement of society (Carayannis et al. 2012). Carayannis et al. (2012) argue that the *Quintuple Helix Model* makes it clear that the implementation of thought and action in sustainability will have a positive impact on the society as a whole. One on the main objective of the *Quintuple Helix* is to enhance *value in society* through the resource of knowledge which is the way to new possibilities and quality of life (Carayannis et al. 2012).

Carayannis et al. (2012) argue that no matter if one state is developed or not and maybe is leading in different field this in the future will depend on their potential to develop new knowledge, know-how and innovation in balance with nature. However, the *Quintuple Helix Model* includes better exchange of knowledge, new know-how, and innovations enables a better solution for the new challenges of sustainable development (Carayannis et al. 2012). Quintuple Helix innovation model, takes natural-environments-of-society as new opportunities for driving further and excelling the sustainable development (Carayannis et al. 2012).

Carayannis et al. (2017), in their paper explore and profile the nature and dynamics of the "Quadruple/**Quintuple** Helix Innovation System Framework as an enabler and enactor of regional co-opetitive entrepreneurial ecosystems conceptualized as fractal, multi-level, multi-modal, multi-nodal, and multi-lateral configurations of dynamic tangible and intangible assets within the resource-based view and the new theory of the growth of the firm."

The main goal of all "helix" models is that universities, business and public-sector organizations all coming together in order to foster innovation and economic prosperity (Parveen et al. 2015). Furthermore, the fourth and fifth helices emphasize the interaction of the triple helix with the civil society and the environment.

Conclusion

In summary, as we highlighted at the literature review, organization is an open system, thus it creates benefits for others but also can use benefits from other. Furthermore, organization should cooperate with others creativity and innovation. As suggested by Chesbrough et al. (2011) companies should find a way to utilize the distributed pools of knowledge possessed by customers, suppliers, universities, national labs, consortia, consultants and even their own competitors. The combination of diverse knowledge increases the chances of finding creative solutions leading to innovations that are more radical. However, this cooperation, or as broadened by MacGregor et al. cooperation, cospecialization, and coopetition between actors, is not straightforward. This chapter brought into light the perspectives that entities, identified as 'helices' in the innovation model, can take in order to achieve the utmost of the synergy that their interaction can bring. This chapter starts with the exploration of the initial model of knowledge production, Triple Helix, representing innovation system model through the interactions of three 'helices' in knowledge production: universities-industry-governments.

Even though Triple Helix brought innovation in the way how companies tended to approach new growth opportunities, the model underwent through more changes. In other words, a new framework of the innovation model was introduced, known as Quadruple Helix (Carayannis and Campbell 2009). The quadruple helix model of innovation involves civil society with business, academia, and government sectors with aim to drive changes (Curley and Salmelin 2013). Even here though, the literature noticed a slight disadvantage, which is the lack of the ecological element. The 'Global Warming Era' characteristics interfered also in the literature of the innovation system framework. As a result, in the approach of the Quintuple Helix innovation model, a new perspective is added, the one of *'natural environments of society'*. One can conclude that the last, but not least, helix identified can be considered as opportunities for driving further and excelling the sustainable development. Furthermore, it can contribute toward the coevolution of knowledge economy, knowledge society, and knowledge democracy (Dubina et al. 2012).

References

Afonso, O., Monteiro, S., & Thompson, M. J. R. (2010). *A growth model for the Quadruple Helix innovation theory* (NIPE Working Paper 12). Braga: Universidade do Minho.

Arnkil, R., Järvensivu, A., Koski, P., & Piirainen, T. (2010). *Exploring quadruple helix outlining user-oriented innovation models.* Tampere: Institute for Social Research, University of Tampere.

Arora, A., & Gambardella, A. (1990). Complementarity and external linkages: The strategies of the large firms in biotechnology. *The Journal of Industrial Economics, 38*(4), 361–379.

Arora, A., Fosfuri, A., & Gambardella, A. (2001). Markets for technology and their implications for corporate strategy. *Industrial and Corporate Change, 10*(2), 419–451.

Bruneel, J., d'Este, P., & Salter, A. (2010). Investigating the factors that diminish the barriers to university–industry collaboration. *Research Policy, 39*(7), 858–868.

Campanella, F., Della Peruta, M. R., Bresciani, S., & Dezi, L. (2017). Quadruple Helix and firms' performance: An empirical verification in Europe. *The Journal of Technology Transfer, 42*(2), 267–284.

Campbell, D. F. J., & Güttel, W. H. (2005). Knowledge production of firms: Research networks and the 'scientification' of business R&D. *International Journal of Technology Management, 31*(1/2), 152–175.

Campbell, D. F. J., Carayannis, E. G., & Güttel, W. H. (2013). Academic firm. In E. G. Carayannis (Ed.), *Encyclopedia of creativity, invention, innovation and entrepreneurship.* New York, NY: Springer.

Carayannis, E. G., & Campbell, D. F. (2009). 'Mode 3' and 'Quadruple Helix': Toward a 21st century fractal innovation ecosystem. *International Journal of Technology Management, 46* (3–4), 201–234.

Carayannis, E. G., & Campbell, D. F. (2011). Open innovation diplomacy and a 21st century fractal research, education and innovation (FREIE) ecosystem: Building on the quadruple and Quintuple Helix innovation concepts and the "mode 3" knowledge production system. *Journal of the Knowledge Economy, 2*(3), 327.

Carayannis, E. G., Barth, T. D., & Campbell, D. F. (2012). The Quintuple Helix innovation model: Global warming as a challenge and driver for innovation. *Journal of Innovation and Entrepreneurship, 1*, 2. https://doi.org/10.1186/2192-5372-1-2.

Carayannis, E. G., Meissner, D., & Edelkina, A. (2017). Targeted innovation policy and practice intelligence (TIP2E): Concepts and implications for theory, policy and practice. *The Journal of Technology Transfer, 42*(3), 460–484.

Chesbrough, H. (2003). The logic of open innovation: Managing intellectual property. *California Management Review, 45*(3), 33–58.

Chesbrough, H. W. (2006). The era of open innovation. *Managing Innovation and Change, 127*(3), 34–41.

Chesbrough, H., & Bogers, M. (2014). Explicating open innovation: Clarifying an emerging paradigm for understanding innovation. In *New frontiers in open innovation* (pp. 3–28). Oxford: Oxford University Press.

Chesbrough, H., Ahern, S., Finn, M., & Guerraz, S. (2006). Business models for technology in the developing world: The role of non-governmental organizations. *California Management Review, 48*(3), 48–61.

Chesbrough, H., Vanhaverbeke, W., Bakici, T., & Lopez-Vega, H. (2011). *Open innovation and public policy in Europe*. London: Science Business Publishing.

Curley, M., & Salmelin, B. (2013). Open innovation 2.0: A new paradigm. *OISPG White Paper*, pp. 1–12.

de Araújo Burcharth, A. L., Knudsen, M. P., & Søndergaard, H. A. (2014). Neither invented nor shared here: The impact and management of attitudes for the adoption of open innovation practices. *Technovation, 34*(3), 149–161.

Dubina, I. N., Carayannis, E. G., & Campbell, D. F. J. (2012). Creativity economy and a crisis of the economy? Coevolution of knowledge, innovation, and creativity, and of the knowledge economy and knowledge society. *Journal of Knowledge Economy, 3*, 1–24. https://doi.org/10.1007/s13132-011-0042-y.

Etzkowitz, H., & Leydesdorff, L. (2000). The dynamics of innovation: From National Systems and "Mode 2" to a Triple Helix of university–industry–government relations. *Research Policy, 29*(2), 109–123.

Ferrary, M. (2011). Specialized organizations and ambidextrous clusters in the open innovation paradigm. *European Management Journal, 29*(3), 181–192.

Gans, J. S., & Stern, S. (2003). The product market and the market for "ideas": Commercialization strategies for technology entrepreneurs. *Research Policy, 32*(2), 333–350.

Gassmann, O., Enkel, E., & Chesbrough, H. (2010). The future of open innovation. *R&D Management, 40*(3), 213–221.

Ingenbleek, P. T. M., & Backus, G. B. C. (2015). Organizing open innovation for sustainability. In A. Brem & É. Viardot (Eds.), *Adoption of innovation*. Cham: Springer.

Kennedy, S., Whiteman, G., & van den Ende, J. (2016). Radical innovation for sustainability: The power of strategy and open innovation. *Long Range Planning, 50*, 712–725.

Leydesdorff, L. (2012). *Journal of the Knowledge Economy, 3*, 25. https://doi.org/10.1007/s13132-011-0049-4.

Leydesdorff, L., & Etzkowitz, H. (1996). Emergence of a Triple Helix of university—industry—government relations. *Science and Public Policy, 23*(5), 279–286.

Leydesdorff, L., & Ivanova, I. (2016). "Open innovation" and "triple helix" models of innovation: Can synergy in innovation systems be measured? *Journal of Open Innovation: Technology, Market, and Complexity, 2*(1), 11.

Melese, T., Lin, S. M., Chang, J. L., & Cohen, N. H. (2009). Open innovation networks between academia and industry: An imperative for breakthrough therapies. *Nature Medicine, 15*(5), 502.

Miller, K., McAdam, R., Moffett, S., Alexander, A., & Puthusserry, P. (2016). Knowledge transfer in university Quadruple Helix ecosystems: An absorptive capacity perspective. *R&D Management, 46*(2), 383–399.

Parveen, S., Senin, A. A., & Umar, A. (2015). Organization culture and open innovation: A Quadruple Helix open innovation model approach. *International Journal of Economics and Financial Issues, 5*(1S), 335–342.

Rauter, R., Perl-Vorbach, E., & Baumgartner, R. J. (2017). Is open innovation supporting sustainable innovation? Findings based on a systematic, explorative analysis of existing literature. *International Journal of Innovation and Sustainable Development, 11*(2–3), 249–270.

Rexhepi, G. (2015). Entering new markets: Strategies for internationalization of family businesses. In *Family businesses in transition economies* (pp. 293–303). Cham: Springer.

Rexhepi, G., & Berisha, B. (2017). The effects of emotional intelligence in managing changes: An entrepreneurial perspective. *World Review of Entrepreneurship, Management and Sustainable Development, 13*(2–3), 237–251.

Rexhepi, G., Ramadani, V., Rahdari, A., & Anggadwita, G. (2017). Models and strategies of family businesses internationalization: A conceptual framework and future research directions. *Review of International Business and Strategy, 27*(2), 248–260.

Sarkar, S., & Costa, A. I. (2008). Dynamics of open innovation in the food industry. *Trends in Food Science & Technology, 19*(11), 574–580.

Schumpeter, J. A. (1942). *Capitalism, socialism and democracy*. New York: Routledge.

Suklev, B., & Rexhepi, G. (2013). Growth strategies of entrepreneurial businesses: Evidence from Macedonia. In *Entrepreneurship in the Balkans* (pp. 77–87). Berlin: Springer.

Syla, S., & Rexhepi, G. (2013). Quality circles: What do they mean and how to implement them? *International Journal of Academic Research in Business and Social Sciences, 3*(12), 243.

Vanhaverbeke, W., Van de Vrande, V., & Chesbrough, H. (2008). Understanding the advantages of open innovation practices in corporate venturing in terms of real options. *Creativity and Innovation Management, 17*(4), 251–258.

Gadaf Rexhepi is Associate Professor at South-East European University, Republic of Macedonia, where he teaches both undergraduate and postgraduate courses in the field of Management. His research interests include innovation, open innovation, strategy, family businesses and sustainability. He authored or co-authored around sixty research articles in different peer and refereed journals and ten text-books among which his later paper on Sustainable Development journal. He is part of many expert's team and have been invited by many organizations as lecturer and trainer. Dr. Rexhepi also has been engaged as advisor of the Minister of Economy in Macedonia. He served as a pro-dean for post-graduate studies 2012–2015. Recently he has been appointed as consultant for development of the Rector of South East European University. He serves on the editorial and review boards of several journals from in the field of entrepreneurship and management. He received the Award for Excellence 2016—Outstanding Paper by Emerald Group Publishing (Journal of Enterprising Communities: People and Places in the Global Economy).

Hyrije Abazi is a Lecturer Assistant of Economics, Quantitative Methods, and Corporate Finance modules at the Faculty of Business and Economics at South-East European University since 2005. She finished her PhD at Staffordshire University in 2013. Her field of research is microeconomics such as ownership change, innovation, gender issues, etc., in transition economies. She has been leading project manager and senior research in United Nations Development Programme (UNDP) and Senior Researcher—Regional Research Promotion Program (RRPP) Project. She has published more than 30 research paper in peer-reviewed journals.

Amir Rahdari is the Director of Sustainability Research Group at USERN, Associate Editor of IJSECSR, and a Sustainability and Social Responsibility Certified Associate (UK). He was selected as one of the TOP25UNDER25 leaders in sustainable business (2degrees, UK) and a Science Sentinel (publons), and he is a member of GBI (US), SSRI (UK), ISDS (Jap.), and two dozen sustainability organizations. His research concerns the sustainability–business intersection with a major focus on sustainable business, sustainability reporting, rating systems, transparency, sustainability indicators, social innovation, and child-focused CSR.

Biljana Angelova since 2006 is head of postgraduate study program in International Management and since 2008 has been head of postgraduate study program in financial management. From 2012 to 2016, she became head of Doctoral Studies on Organizational Science—Management, at the Ss. Cyril and Methodius University in Skopje. In November 2009, she was nominated for the position of deputy director of the Institute of Economics, and since 2010 until September 2016, she was a director of the Institute of Economics. Since 2016, she is Vice-Rector for finance, investments, and development at the "Ss. Cyril and Methodius University" in Skopje.

Investigating the Effect of Inbound and Outbound Open Innovation on Discovery and Exploiting of Entrepreneurial Opportunities

Ali Davari, Amir Emami, and Seyedmohammadhossein Seyedi

Abstract One of the critical factors contributes to the success of firms, in competitive world, is innovation. Open innovation offers many benefits to enterprises as cost reduction, NPD, accelerating the production of new products and services. Open innovation produces more market knowledge and new technologies. As a result, firms do better in discovering and exploiting opportunities. This paper investigates the effect of inbound and outbound open innovation on the discovery and exploitation of entrepreneurial opportunities. Based on theoretical studies, nine indicators for inbound open innovation and six indicators for outbound open innovation were selected. Subsequently, a questionnaire was distributed among 83 SMEs in the field of IT. The results show that only a small number of inbound and outbound open innovation indicators have a positive impact on the discovery and exploitation of entrepreneurial opportunities.

Introduction

Studies show that the traditional approach to innovation is not sufficient for today's competitive environment. In the past, enterprises were implementing most of their innovative activities within and protecting their innovations as a strategic asset. In closed innovation, firms have been controlling the innovation and R&D processes.

Increasing global competition, firms need to learn from others through more interaction (Väätänen et al. 2011).

According to close innovation, firms should develop their ideas, enter them into the market and seek financial support based on internal control. Then they sell the product through the channel and provide after-sales services. So, firms tend to

A. Davari · S. Seyedi
Faculty of Entrepreneurship, University of Tehran, Tehran, Iran
e-mail: ali_davari@ut.ac.ir; mr.m.seyedi@ut.ac.ir

A. Emami (✉)
Faculty of Management, Kharazmi University, Tehran, Iran
e-mail: a.emami@khu.ac.ir

© Springer Nature Switzerland AG 2019
G. Rexhepi et al. (eds.), *Open Innovation and Entrepreneurship*,
https://doi.org/10.1007/978-3-030-16912-1_4

behave in the framework of a closed architecture (Chesbrough 2006a, b). In close innovation, the emphasis is on recruiting talent individuals in the firm, discovering, developing and exploiting internal R&D to profit, commercializing innovation within the company, and maintaining the IP of internal ideas. While open innovation is based on using the knowledge of talent people outside the company, the simultaneous use of both internal and external R&D, the use of internal and external ideas, and IP sales (Dufour and Son 2015).

Open innovation has been highly regarded due to of short cycle of innovation (Gassmann and Enkel 2005), cost reduction of innovation (Felin and Zenger 2014), cost reduction of developing new products (Lapointe and Guimont 2015; Felin and Zenger 2014), and reduction of time to market (Van de Vrande et al. 2009). Technology Changes help to share risks among firms in the new products development and improve brand reputation.

The application of open innovation in the commercialization process by firms has many benefits. For example, according to studies, the use of open innovation can increase the product's success rate up to 50% and increase the profit of internal R&D up to 60% (Enkel et al. 2009).

The entry into innovation era has increased the access to skilled labor, venture capital, external choices for new ideas and external suppliers. Open innovation paradigm may increase different flows, such as supply chain management, strategic alliances, networks, learning, and discovery and exploitation (van de Vrande and De Man 2011). Close innovation cause challenges in financing, developing new ideas, getting access to channels of new markets, and meeting the expectations and needs of potential and actual customers, technology development, exploiting ideas and gaining their competitive advantage, identifying new opportunities for profitability, obtaining externally acquired knowledge, gaining outcomes and complementary outsourcing capabilities in twenty-first century (Reed et al. 2012). Besides, the benefits of open innovation, firms involved in the process of open innovation, face some problems and barriers. Research on 107 European firms shows that factors such as loss of knowledge (48%), high coordination costs (48%), higher complexity, and loss of control (a total of 41%) are the most common risks of open innovation. In addition, finding the appropriate partner (43%), coordination between open innovation activities and other day-to-day activities (36%), allocating resources and time to open innovation activities, are the most critical internal barriers to implement open innovation activities (Enkel and Gassmann 2008).

Recent studies of OI emphasis on external cooperation, degree of OI, type of industries (manufacturing/service) (Jacobfeuerborn 2014), intensity of technology (High Tech industries/Low Tech industries), market (domestic markets/foreign markets) and the size of the company (large/small or medium) (G. Abulrub and Lee 2012; Van de Vrande et al. 2009; Chesbrough and Crowther 2006). Studies show that Large-scale firms tend to focus on R&D, while SMEs focus mainly on commercialization, because of lower production capacity, lower availability of distribution channels and communications to introduce their innovations effectively (Sungjoo Lee et al. 2010).

Meanwhile, the level of open innovation adoption by firms depends on the level of economic and technological development of countries. This phenomenon is also related to the national innovation system of countries. There are examples of open innovation in developing countries (Lee et al. 2012). Industries that are technologically advanced and technological advancements are faster in them, tend to be more open to innovation, knowledge sharing and technology absorption (Bigliardi et al. 2012). Nevertheless, researches of this area are limited due to early stages studies (Abulrub and Lee 2012).

This paper aims to determine the role of open innovation in the discovery and exploitation of entrepreneurial opportunities. So far, there has been no research among Iranian firms measuring the impact of open innovation (inbound vs. outbound) on the discovery and exploitation of entrepreneurial opportunities. As a result, to investigate the issue, firstly, the literature on inbound and outbound innovation is reviewed. Secondly, the discovery and exploitation of entrepreneurial opportunities are discussed. Thirdly, building on extant research, the dimensions of the conceptual model of research are introduced. Fourthly, the hypotheses of research are presented. Then, the research data is analyzed through statistical software and system dynamics. Finally, we discuss the results of the research in more details.

Literature

Entering the twenty-first century, a shift has been occurred in the commercialization of industrial knowledge of firms so that some firms are forced to move from the twentieth-century model of innovation to a new paradigm of innovation. Henry Chesbrough initially introduced open innovation concept in 2003. Chesbrough's studies (2003, 2006a, b) showed that the presentation of innovative ideas and commercialization methods have been changed. He defined open innovation as "deliberate use of internal and external knowledge to increase the speed of domestic innovation and expand the market for external use of innovation." Most closed innovation was created in the departments of a firm, while open innovation is concentrated on networks and made up of different firms and related sections in the firm (Won Park et al. 2012). Table 1 summarizes the list of features Shows both paradigms.

Therefore, open innovation is a paradigm in which firms or businesses can use external ideas in addition to internal ideas (Monsef and Wan Ismail 2012). Open innovation paradigm shapes an antithesis of the traditional vertical integration model. Innovation models highlight the interactive features of innovation and show that firms need to engage with users, suppliers, competitors and associates and an internal department of innovation (Monsef and Wan Ismail 2012).

Previously, other authors have introduced the concept of absorption capacity. The concept of knowledge absorption capacity is, in fact, the organization's learning from the environment; learning that focuses on knowledge sources in the environment instead of emphasizing the transfer of knowledge through organization experience. If organizational learning approaches are divided into two types of individual and collective, the knowledge absorption capacity from the environment

Table 1 Comparisons of open innovation and close innovation

Open innovation	Close innovation
Hiring the knowledge of talents outside the firm	Hiring talents to work in the firm
The simultaneous exploitation of domestic and external R&D	Discover, develop and exploit internal R&D to earn profits
For the benefit of ideas, we do not need to form them internally	Commercialization of ideas discovered by the company itself
Best exploitation of internal and external ideas for criteria of success	The most and best internal ideas as a criterion for success
Buying and selling intellectual properties for success	Maintaining the intellectual property of internal ideas

Source: Dufour and Son (2015)

is a person-centered perspective (DeFillippi and Ornstein 2003). In this view, there is an objective knowledge that exists outside the minds of individuals and can be easily transferred to the learner (Gherardi et al. 1998) and learning as a process of transferring information from a knowledge source to a person who does not have the information. As it is seen, absorption capacity is more interpersonal while open innovation is more organizational.

The principal motivations of firms to engage in open innovation are achieving new business opportunities, sharing and reducing risk, utilizing complementary resources, and realizing co-operation. Firms use open innovation as a strategic tool to search for new situations at lower risk. The two primary knowledge flows in the open innovation include outside-in and inside-out processes.

- **Outside-in processes** (inbound): using external resources through the acquisition of external knowledge of customers, suppliers or partners, transfer of technologies from other firms (Gassmann and Enkel 2004). Gathering ideas and knowledge to firms through R&D contracts, cooperation with universities, licensing from other firms, ownership and forward and backward integrations (Chesbrough and Crowther 2006), acquiring knowledge through suppliers, customers, or other market actors (Gassmann et al. 2010), collaboration, outsourcing (Michelino et al. 2014). Cooperating with universities and research centers, consultants, clients, suppliers and competitors (Bigliardi et al. 2012). Analyzing customer perspective, collaboration, innovation networks, innovation intermediation, intellectual property, or technology licenses from other firms or their ownership (Emami and Talebi 2011).

- **Inside-out processes** (outbound): Some think that open innovation is merely outside-in, while open innovation can flow inside-out. Inside-out flow contributes to use unused knowledge in businesses. This dimension of open innovations is often hidden (Chesbrough 2017). This process involves the external use of internal ideas from, IP sales and the transfer of ideas to the external environment. High-tech firms focus on the use of inside-out process to reduce the cost of R&D and the transfer of innovation risk (Gassmann and Enkel 2004), transfer of technology, ideas and knowledge to external firms and licensing other firms, investing in spin-off (Chesbrough and Crowther 2006), the transfer of internal

Table 2 Dimensions of open innovation in different researches

Dimensions		Van de Vrande et al. (2009)	Bigliardi and Galati (2016)	Schroll and Mild (2011)	Chesbrough and Brunswicker (2013)	Chesbrough and Brunswicker (2014)
Inbound OI	External consultants			✓		
	Employee involvement					
	Customers involvement	✓	✓	✓	✓	✓
	Suppliers	✓		✓		✓
	Competitors			✓	✓	
	IP in and licencing	✓	✓		✓	✓
	Networking	✓	✓		✓	✓
	Universities		✓		✓	
	R&D in		✓		✓	
Outbound OI	Joint venture				✓	✓
	Participations in standardizations				✓	
	Venture capital with external partners	✓				
	Spin off				✓	✓
	R&D out	✓				
	IP out licencing and patent selling	✓	✓	✓	✓	✓
	Selling of market ready products				✓	✓

ideas to outside the company and the sale of intellectual property (Gassmann et al. 2010) can be seen as examples of inside-out open innovation.

In addition to inbound and outbound open innovation, the third stream is presented as a coupled process (Gassmann et al. 2010; Gassmann and Enkel 2004). This third approach implies that firms combine to maximize the value of outside-in and inside-out flows both together (see Table 2).

It should be noted that the application of the open innovation approach is affected by the content and context of firms. Innovation management is different regarding external factors such as industry type, type of innovation, the developmental extent of the country. In other words, acceptance of open innovation models is influenced by the internal and external factors of the company and industry. Based on various models, the factors that affect the implementation of open innovation are identified as follows:

- General environmental factors: technological, economic, cultural, political and legal
- Specific environmental factors: competition, partner, size, industry users or consumers (Mergel 2017).

- Internal factors: business model, organization structure, organization culture, leadership commitment, employee engagement (Elmquist et al. 2009; Emami et al. 2019a), change management and management of external organizational communications (Chesbrough and Brunswicker 2014), and openness versus closeness.

Open innovation process ranges from low to high (Chaston and Scott 2012), as firms in this spectrum are high, they use external resources to innovate more.

Discovering and Exploiting Opportunities

Opportunity is a process in which we seek to create or deliver value to beneficiaries (Ardichvili et al. 2003).The process of opportunity can be divided into two section of discovery and exploitation of opportunities. Discovery and exploitation of opportunities may lead to the production of goods and services, raw materials, modified or new processes (Shane and Venkataraman 2000). Discovery of opportunities implies the capacity to recognize, analyze the needs of society and industry, analyze the business environment, transfer of knowledge flow.

There are several ways to recognize opportunities, such as active search, random search, and forth. The exploitation of opportunities refers to the patterns that entrepreneurs or firms take advantage of opportunities. Knowledge commercializing, networking, managing relationships with partners are essential in exploiting opportunities.

According to Van de Vrande et al. (2009), open innovation can help to discover and exploit technology. Discovery involves (1) Customer involvement in the innovation process (active research in the market to identify their needs, or develop products based on customer demands). (2) External networking: relying on collaboration with outside partners in the network to support the innovative process. (3) External participation: stock-based investments in a new or existing business for access to knowledge for synergy. (4) Inward IP licensing, such as the purchase of patents, copyrights, or trademarks owned by other firms to the benefit of foreign knowledge. (5) Outsourcing R&D: purchasing R&D services from other firms such as universities, government research centers, private sector suppliers (Van de Vrande et al. 2009). The exploitation includes (1) Venturing based on internal knowledge, domestic financing, domestic human capital, and other resources within the business. (2) Outward IP licensing, selling intellectual property to other firms for better exploitation of opportunities, such as patents, publishing rights, and trademarks. (3) Employee involvement: Using knowledge and initiatives of employees who are not directly engaged in R&D activities.

Open innovation leads to an increase in market knowledge as well as in technology. As a result, firms do better at discovering and exploiting opportunities. In small and medium-sized enterprises or SMEs, innovation processes are made more quickly due to their higher flexibility, faster decision-making speeds, and faster reaction to market changes by them (Emami et al. 2019b; Vanhaverbeke 2006). By expanding external corporate communications, discovering and exploiting opportunities contribute to increase new commercialization of products, entrance the new markets, using new technology, new materials, new resources, and new production method.

As discussed above, the use of open innovation approaches to both the inside and outside influence the discovery and exploitation of entrepreneurial opportunities. Therefore, the paper examines the impact of open innovation approaches in discovering and exploiting entrepreneurial opportunities.

Research Conceptual Model

In the paper, innovation is divided into two types: internal and external. The research is conducted in small and medium enterprises. Since SMEs context is often used for the inbound and outbound open innovation, we use it as the context of this study. The dimensions of inbound and outbound open innovation were considered. These dimensions are presented in Table 3.

Table 3 Definition and dimensions of inbound and outbound OI

Dimensions		Definition
Inbound OI	External consultants	Temporary recruitment of outside specialists
	Employee involvement	Using employee knowledge through programs such as suggestion systems and independent work teams
	Customers involvement	Involving customers in innovative processes through market research or product development based on their feedbacks
	Suppliers	Collaboration with suppliers in order to transfer customer needs to them or get ideas from them
	Competitors	Collaborate with competitors to exchange information and produce common products
	IP in and licensing	Purchase property rights include: License for the exploitation of technologies, patents, copyright
	Networking	Knowledge sharing with other firms and forums or events informally
	Universities	Contact with universities and colleges
	R&D in	Providing R&D services to other firms
Outbound OI	Joint venture	Joint venture investment with external partners
	Participations in standardizations	Participation in standardization and assessing activities formally and informally
	Venture capital with external partners	A venture capital investment with an ambiguous future
	Spin-off	Establishing new knowledge-based firms and supporting them through foremost firms
	R&D out	Getting R&D services from other firms such as research and testing centers
	IP out licensing and patent selling	Selling licensing right to use inventions and copyrights to other firms for more profit from intellectual properties
	Selling of market ready products	Selling of market-ready products to the third-party to sell to customers

As stated above, open innovation can help firms recognize market requirements and new technologies. It also helps them discover and exploit opportunities. Therefore, the research hypotheses are as below

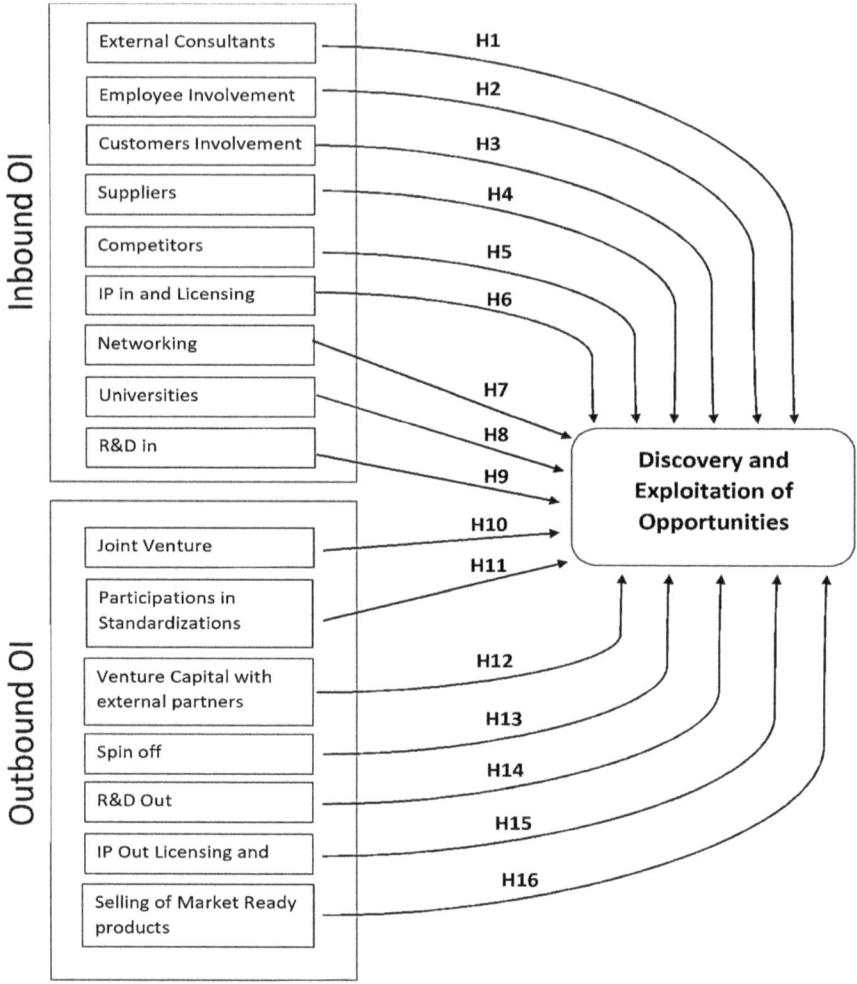

Conceptual model of research

Methodology

The study uses a descriptive-correlation method. The research tool for collecting data is the questionnaire which was extracted from open innovation studies. The questionnaire was distributed among SMEs, and finally, 83 questionnaires were collected from information technology businesses. For analysis of data, SPSS software was used. Alpha Cronbach's questionnaire is above 0.7. In data analysis, the correlation coefficient calculated between dimensions of the conceptual model. To test hypotheses, linear regression coefficients were used. In the next step, multiple regression analysis was used step by step.

In this paper, in addition to the presented methodology, dynamic modeling is used to illustrate the relationships that have been achieved. Dynamic system models help researchers to display interactions between the various parameters of the subject (Sterman 2000). The system dynamics approach was introduced in the early 60's by MIT as a modeling and simulation method for evaluating decision making in the most popular industrial environments.

Results

Pearson, correlation coefficient test, was used to evaluate the relationship between variables (Table 4). As can be seen from results, discovery and exploitation of opportunities have a meaningful relationship with only a few variables of inbound and outbound open innovation.

Linear regression test was run to evaluate acceptance or rejection of the hypotheses h. The results showed that some of the dimensions of inbound and outbound open innovation (independent variables) have a significant effect on the discovery and exploitation of opportunities (Sig. ≤ 0.05 and values $1.96 \leq t$). Table 5 shows the results.

Regression test results showed that the following variables have a positive effect on discovery and exploitation of opportunities.

- Customers Involvement
- Suppliers
- Competitors
- Networking
- Joint Venture
- Spin-off
- Selling of Market Ready products

In the following table, multiple linear regression was used with the stepwise method.

In the stepwise method, the variables rank according to their importance in the models and enter based on their proportion in prediction of dependent variable. The results show that the following indices entered into the model regarding their importance. As shown in Table 5, only three variables are entered into the model

1. Competitors
2. Suppliers
3. Customers Involvement

Table 4 Coefficient matrix for variables

	Mean	1	2	3	4	5	6	7	8	9	10	11	12	13	14	15	16	17
Discovery and exploitation of opportunities	3.18	1.00																
External consultants	2.49	0.18	1.00															
Customers involvement	2.95	0.316**	0.294**	1.00														
Suppliers	3.45	0.257*	0.20	0.15	1.00													
Competitors	2.53	0.333**	0.11	0.19	0.01	1.00												
IP in and licencing	2.65	0.18	0.13	-0.06	0.19	0.15	1.00											
Networking	3.14	0.232*	0.00	0.10	-0.04	0.304**	0.13	1.00										
Employee involvement	3.17	0.18	0.21	0.17	0.20	0.271*	0.224*	0.08	1.00									
Universities	2.65	0.06	0.06	-0.09	0.05	0.13	0.02	-0.08	0.19	1.00								
R&D in	3.22	0.11	-0.295**	-0.228*	0.04	0.11	-0.03	0.340**	0.00	0.02	1.00							
Joint venture	2.70	0.472**	0.13	0.456**	0.307**	0.254*	0.12	0.373**	0.336**	-0.243*	-0.15	1.00						
Participations in standardizations	3.17	0.03	-0.312*	-0.241*	0.16	0.17	0.273*	0.20	-0.03	0.307**	0.258*	-0.01	1.00					
Venture capital with external partners	3.31	0.11	-0.14	-0.19	-0.07	0.12	0.243*	0.456**	0.07	0.09	0.337**	0.04	0.15	1.00				
Spin off	2.86	0.284**	-0.03	0.19	0.16	-0.05	-0.05	0.20	0.230*	0.12	0.10	0.409**	0.02	0.10	1.00			
R&D out	3.29	0.10	-0.03	-0.05	0.598**	0.20	0.07	-0.01	0.13	0.08	0.239*	0.16	0.363**	0.04	0.341**	1.00		
IP out licencing and patent selling	3.13	-0.03	0.238*	-0.07	0.09	0.18	0.04	0.294**	0.20	0.04	0.226*	0.03	-0.08	0.15	0.275*	0.13	1.00	
Selling of market ready products	2.82	0.382**	-0.09	0.09	0.234*	0.13	-0.15	0.15	-0.19	0.08	0.337**	0.01	0.12	-0.01	0.337**	0.230*	0.03	1.00

$P < 0.05*$ and $0.01**$

Table 5 Linear regression results

Hypothesis		Model summary		Anova		Coefficients			Result
		R	R2	F	Sig.	Beta	t	Sig.	
H1.1.	External consultants→D.E.	0.18	0.03	2.60	0.11	0.13	1.61	0.11	Reject
2	Employee involvement→D.E.	0.18	0.03	2.72	0.10	0.18	1.65	0.10	Reject
3	Customers involvement→D.E.	0.32	0.10	8.96	0.00	0.32	2.99	0.00	Accept
4	Suppliers→D.E.	0.26	0.07	5.74	0.02	0.26	2.40	0.02	Accept
5	Competitors→D.E.	0.33	0.11	10.07	0.00	0.33	3.17	0.00	Accept
6	IP in and licensing→D.E.	0.18	0.03	2.83	0.10	0.18	1.68	0.10	Reject
7	Networking→D.E.	0.23	0.05	4.59	0.04	0.23	2.14	0.04	Accept
8	Universities→D.E.	0.06	0.00	0.32	0.57	0.06	0.57	0.57	Reject
9	R&D in→D.E.	0.11	0.01	0.90	0.34	0.11	0.95	0.34	Reject
10	Joint venture→D.E.	0.47	0.22	23.24	0.00	0.47	4.82	0.00	Accept
11	Participations in standardizations→D.E.	0.03	0.00	0.08	0.78	0.03	0.28	0.78	Reject
12	Venture capital with external partners→D.E.	0.11	0.01	1.03	0.31	0.11	1.02	0.31	Reject
13	Spin off→D.E.	0.28	0.08	7.10	0.01	0.28	2.67	0.01	Accept
14	R&D out→D.E.	0.10	0.01	0.78	0.38	0.10	0.88	0.38	Reject
15	IP out licensing and patent selling→D.E.	0.03	0.00	0.09	0.77	−0.03	−0.29	0.77	Reject
16	Selling of market ready products→D.E.	0.38	0.15	13.87	0.00	0.38	3.72	0.00	Accept

Table 6 Multiple linear regressions by stepwise method

Model	Independent variable (Inbound OI)	Model summary			ANOVA		Coefficients		
		R	R^2	Adj. R^2	F	Sig.	Beta	t	Sig.
1	Competitors	0.34	0.11	0.1	9.91	0.00	0.34	3.15	0.00
2	Competitors	0.43	0.18	0.16	8.64	0.00	0.34	3.28	0.00
	Suppliers						0.27	2.58	0.00
3	Competitors	0.48	0.23	0.2	7.38	0.00	0.29	2.76	0.00
	Suppliers						0.22	2.12	0.04
	Customers involvement						0.22	2.04	0.05

In the first model, the competitors entered with Adjusted R^2 0.11 (Table 6). In the second model, the Suppliers entered which together with the competitors explain entire 18% of the dependent variables.

In the last model, by entering the customer's involvement, Adjusted R Square reached 0.23. These three variables determine 23% of the variations in discovery and exploitation of opportunities. Removing other variables implies that the interactive effect of independent variables has led to the neutralization of the effect of other variables. Also, the low Adjusted R Square in models suggests that the

Table 7 Multiple linear regressions by stepwise method

Model	Independent variable (Outbound OI)	Model summary			Anova		Coefficients		
		R	R^2	Adj. R^2	F	Sig.	Beta	t	Sig.
1	Joint venture	0.47	0.22	0.21	23.24	0.00	0.47	4.82	0.00
2	Joint venture	0.61	0.37	0.35	23.07	0.00	0.47	5.26	0.00
	Selling of market ready products						0.38	4.25	0.00

open inbound innovation has little effect on recognizing and exploiting entrepreneurial opportunities.

Additionally, meaningful indicators of outbound open innovation were introduced into the model. The results indicate that the following indices are in the order of importance entered into the model. As shown in Table 7, only two variables are entered into the model.

1. Joint Venture
2. Selling of Market Ready products

In the first model, the joint venture has entered into the model (Adjusted R^2) 0.21. In the second model, Selling of market-ready products entered which together with joint venture explains a total of 0.35 of the dependent variables. In total, these two variables determine 35% of the changes in discovery and exploitation of the opportunity. As explained above, removing other variables implies that the interactive effect of independent variables has led to the neutralization of the effect of this variable.

Figure 1 shows an overview of the causal relationships between the primary variables of open innovation that affects the discovery and exploitation of opportunities.

Discussion and Conclusion

The emergence of open innovation helps firms to move beyond internal boundaries and, through the creation of mechanisms, strive to develop and maintain cooperation with other firms. The familiarity of firms with this concept and its benefits will lead to choosing the partners, increasing the ability to use supplementary resources and reducing financial risks in the new products or services development.

This paper examined the impact of inbound and outbound open innovation on the discovery and exploitation of entrepreneurial opportunities in the Iranian IT based SMEs.

Indicators that have been investigated in inbound OI open innovation process include external consultants, employee involvement, customers involvement, suppliers, competitors, IP in and licensing, networking, universities and R&D. Indicators of Outbound OI process comprise joint venture, participation in standardizations,

Fig. 1 Causal relationship

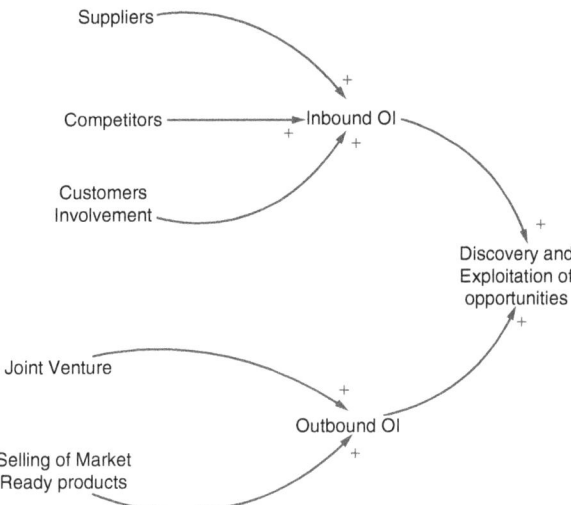

venture capital with external partners, spin-off, R&D out IP Licensing and patent selling and selling of market-ready products.

Investigating the effect of inbound and outbound parameters on discovering and exploiting opportunities, it has been shown that customers involvement, suppliers, competitors, networking, joint venture, spin-off and selling of market-ready products have a significant effect on the discovery and exploitation of opportunities (Sig. ≤ 0.05 and values $1.96 \leq t$). It is observed that most of inbound and outbound open innovation parameters do not affect the discovery and exploitation of opportunities. The R^2 explanation reflects the weak effect of these parameters on the discovery and exploitation of opportunities. It means open innovation may not shape opportunities powerfully in these firms. It can be said that the internal structure of the firms has a significant impact on open innovation. Previous studies have shown that the processes of open innovation in SMEs prove much faster due to their higher flexibility, faster decision-making speeds, and faster response to market changes. However, consistent with Vanhaverbeke (2006) these SMEs face limitations such as human resources, finance, and raw materials.

Based on the model presented by the dynamic system, any increase or decrease in suppliers, competitors and customers involvement parameters will increase or decrease the inbound open innovation. On the other hand, any increase or decrease in inbound open innovation will increase or decrease the discovery and exploitation of opportunity. Also, any increase or decrease in joint Venture and selling of market-ready products parameters will increase or decrease the outbound open innovation. On the other hand, any increase or decrease in outbound open innovation will increase or decrease the discovery and exploitation of opportunity.

It should be noted that the relationship between inbound and outbound OI, and the process of discovery and exploiting the opportunity, is not a quick and cross-sectional relationship. In other words, it is expected that after improving the corporate environment (whether inbound open innovation and outbound open innovation), and with a time lag, discovery and exploitation processes can significantly improve/diminish.

Furthermore, firms will be redirected to innovations by observing performance improvements in the process of recognizing and exploiting opportunities, which will result in a continuous improvement cycle for firms. Accordingly, it is suggested that more research should be done to identify the results and performance of open innovation with a longitudinal research approach. For example, future research can investigate the effect of inbound and outbound open innovation on the degree of innovation of opportunities (Emami and Dimov 2017) and exploitation.

References

Abulrub, A. H. G., & Lee, J. (2012). Open innovation management: Challenges and prospects. *Procedia-Social and Behavioral Sciences, 41*, 130–138.

Ardichvili, A., Cardozo, R., & Ray, S. (2003). A theory of entrepreneurial opportunity identification and development. *Journal of Business Venturing, 18*(1), 105–123.

Bigliardi, B., & Galati, F. (2016). Which factors hinder the adoption of open innovation in SMEs? *Technology Analysis & Strategic Management, 28*(8), 869–885.

Bigliardi, B., Ivo Dormio, A., & Galati, F. (2012). The adoption of open innovation within the telecommunication industry. *European Journal of Innovation Management, 15*(1), 27–54.

Chaston, I., & Scott, G. J. (2012). Entrepreneurship and open innovation in an emerging economy. *Management Decision, 50*(7), 1161–1177.

Chesbrough, H. (2003). *Open innovation: The new imperative for creating and profiting from technology*. Boston, MA: Harvard Business School Press.

Chesbrough, H. (2006a). Open innovation: A new paradigm for understanding industrial innovation. *Open Innovation: Researching A New Paradigm, 400*, 0–19.

Chesbrough, H. W. (2006b). *Open innovation: The new imperative for creating and profiting from technology*. Boston, MA: Harvard Business Press.

Chesbrough, H. (2017). The future of open innovation: The future of open innovation is more extensive, more collaborative, and more engaged with a wider variety of participants. *Research-Technology Management, 60*(1), 35–38.

Chesbrough, H., & Brunswicker, S. (2013). Managing open innovation in large firms, Survey report. *Executive survey on open innovation [interaktyvus]*, 6.

Chesbrough, H., & Brunswicker, S. (2014). A fad or a phenomenon?: The adoption of open innovation practices in large firms. *Research-Technology Management, 57*(2), 16–25.

Chesbrough, H., & Crowther, A. K. (2006). Beyond high tech: Early adopters of open innovation in other industries. *R&D Management, 36*(3), 229–236.

DeFillippi, R., & Ornstein, S. (2003). Psychological perspectives underlying theories of organizational learning. In *The Blackwell handbook of organizational learning and knowledge management* (pp. 19–35). Oxford, Blackwell.

Dufour, J., & Son, P. E. (2015). Open innovation in SMEs–towards formalization of openness. *Journal of Innovation Management, 3*(3), 90.

Elmquist, M., Fredberg, T., & Ollila, S. (2009). Exploring the field of open innovation. *European Journal of Innovation Management, 12*(3), 326–345.

Emami, A., & Dimov, D. (2017). Degree of innovation and the entrepreneurs' intention to create value: A comparative study of experienced and novice entrepreneurs. *Eurasian Business Review, 7*(2), 161–182.

Emami, A., & Talebi, K. (2011). Decision framing and critical success factors of new product development. *African Journal of Business Management, 5*, 6233–6239.

Emami, A., Molaie, M., & Khajehian, D. (2019a). Does employee innovation mediate the relationship between employee performance and relationship marketing? An ICT-based case. *World Review of Entrepreneurship, Management and Sustainable Development.* (In press).

Emami, A., Welsh, D., Ramadani, V., & Davari, A. (2019b). The impact of judgment and framing on entrepreneurs' decision making. *Journal of Small Business and Entrepreneurship.* https://doi.org/10.1080/08276331.2018.1551461. (In press).

Enkel, E., & Gassmann, O. (2008). *Driving open innovation in the front end.* The IBM case, Working Paper, University of St. Gallen/Zeppelin University, St Gallen/Friedrichshafen.

Enkel, E., Gassmann, O., & Chesbrough, H. (2009). Open R&D and open innovation: Exploring the phenomenon. *R&D Management, 39*(4), 311–316.

Felin, T., & Zenger, T. R. (2014). Closed or open innovation? Problem solving and the governance choice. *Research Policy, 43*(5), 914–925.

Gassmann, O., & Enkel, E. (2004). *Towards a theory of open innovation: Three core process archetypes.* Proceedings of the R&D Management Conference, 6–9 July 2004, Lisbon, Portugal.

Gassmann, O., & Enkel, E. (2005). Open Innovation Forschung. Forschungsfragen und erste Erkenntnisse. In M. A. Weissenberger-Eibl (Ed.), *Gestaltung von Innovationssystemen.* Kassel: Cactus Group Verlag.

Gassmann, O., Enkel, E., & Chesbrough, H. (2010). The future of open innovation. *R&D Management, 40*(3), 213–221.

Gherardi, S., Nicolini, D., & Odella, F. (1998). Toward a social understanding of how people learn in organizations: The notion of situated curriculum. *Management Learning, 29*(3), 273–297.

Jacobfeuerborn, B. (2014). An informational model of open innovation. In *Intelligent tools for building a scientific information platform: From research to implementation* (pp. 15–24). Cham: Springer.

Lapointe, D., & Guimont, D. (2015). Open innovation practices adopted by private stakeholders: Perspectives for living labs. *Info, 17*(4), 67–80.

Lee, S., Park, G., Yoon, B., & Park, J. (2010). Open innovation in SMEs—An intermediated network model. *Research Policy, 39*(2), 290–300.

Lee, S. M., Hwang, T., & Choi, D. (2012). Open innovation in the public sector of leading countries. *Management Decision, 50*(1), 147–162.

Mergel, I. (2017). Open innovation in the public sector: Drivers and barriers for the adoption of Challenge.gov. *Public Management Review,* 1–20.

Michelino, F., Caputo, M., Cammarano, A., & Lamberti, E. (2014). Inbound and outbound open innovation: Organization and performances. *Journal of Technology Management & Innovation, 9*(3), 65–82.

Monsef, S., & Ismail, W. K. W. (2012). The impact of open innovation in new product development process. *International Journal of Fundamental Psychology & Social Sciences, 2*(1), 7–12.

Reed, R., Storrud-Barnes, S., & Jessup, L. (2012). How open innovation affects the drivers of competitive advantage: Trading the benefits of IP creation and ownership for free invention. *Management Decision, 50*(1), 58–73.

Schroll, A., & Mild, A. (2011). Open innovation modes and the role of internal R&D: An empirical study on open innovation adoption in Europe. *European Journal of Innovation Management, 14*(4), 475–495.

Shane, S., & Venkataraman, S. (2000). The promise of entrepreneurship as a field of research. *Academy of Management Review, 25*(1), 217–226.

Sterman, J. D. (2000). *Business dynamics: Systems thinking and modeling for a complex world* (No. HD30. 2 S7835 2000).

Väätänen, J., Podmetina, D., Savitskaya, I., & Torkkeli, M. (2011). New trends in Russian innovations: The ownership effect on the adoption of open innovation practices. *Journal of East-West Business, 17*(2–3), 132–143.

van de Vrande, V., & de Man, A. P. (2011). A response to "Is open innovation a field of study or a communication barrier to theory development?". *Technovation, 31*(4), 185–186.

Van de Vrande, V., De Jong, J. P., Vanhaverbeke, W., & De Rochemont, M. (2009). Open innovation in SMEs: Trends, motives and management challenges. *Technovation, 29*(6–7), 423–437.

Vanhaverbeke, W. (2006). The interorganizational context of open innovation. In *Open innovation: Researching a new paradigm* (pp. 205–219). Oxford: Oxford University Press.

Won Park, Y., Amano, T., & Moon, G. (2012). Benchmarking open and cluster innovation: Case of Korea. *Benchmarking: An International Journal, 19*(4/5), 517–531.

Ali Davari is an Assistant professor at the Faculty of Entrepreneurship, University of Tehran. His research interests are entrepreneurship policy, national competitiveness, institutions, country-level analysis, and corporate entrepreneurship. He has authored three books and around 30 papers on entrepreneurship. Dr. Davari is a member of some business creation committees such as the Business Creation Committee of the Management and Planning Organization of Iran.

Amir Emami is an Assistant Professor of Entrepreneurship and Strategy at the Faculty of Management, Kharazmi University (Iran). His research interests lie in the intersection of cognition, value creation, and entrepreneurship. In his research, he explores some of the most important factors that impact value creation in the course of entrepreneurial opportunity development. His works have appeared in *International Small Business Journal, International Entrepreneurship and Management Journal, Eurasian Business Review*, and *Advances in Production Engineering and Management*.

Seyedmohammadhossein Seyedi is an entrepreneurship student at the University of Tehran. He is interested in the simulation of systems and innovation. He is an expert in simulation software such as Vensim. Based on uncertainty in innovation and entrepreneurship issues, his master thesis is about simulation of TIS (Technology Information System—narrowing down in Nanotechnology). He has worked as a member of the innovation team in Mofid Securities for 2 years. His efforts have led to some novelties in financial markets in Iran.

The Role of Industry and Economic Context in Open Innovation

Abiodun Egbetokun, Omolayo Oluwatope, David Adeyeye, and Maruf Sanni

Abstract Using innovation survey data on a sample of UK manufacturing firms, Laursen and Salter (Open for innovation: The role of openness in explaining innovation performance among UK manufacturing firms. Strategic Management Journal, 27:131–150, 2006) documented a non-monotonous relationship between external search strategies and firm-level innovative performance. We find partially similar results in a combined sample of Nigerian manufacturing and service firms. A major discrepancy is that external search appears not to matter for radical innovation in our sample. Based on multiple research streams including economics of innovation and development economics, we develop and test new hypotheses on sectoral differences and the role of the economic context. We find that in a developing context, a wider range of innovation obstacles implies broader external search and more intense obstacles require deeper search. We explore the implications of these results for management research and theory.

Introduction

Innovation is a systemic phenomenon that is strongly related to the use of external knowledge (Tomlinson 2010; Enkel et al. 2009; Chesbrough 2003; Lundvall 1988). There are two well-known empirical regularities on this relationship, as demonstrated by extensive research evidence. The first one is based on the seminal work of Cohen and Levinthal (1989, 1990) on absorptive capacity. A firm tends to be more or less innovative depending on its ability to appropriate external knowledge (Lin et al. 2012; de Jong and Freel 2010; Todorova and Durisin 2007; Lane et al. 2002, 2006; Zahra and George 2002; Lane and Lubatkin 1998). The second empirical regularity, which builds upon the first, stems from the groundbreaking work of Laursen and

A. Egbetokun (✉) · O. Oluwatope · D. Adeyeye · M. Sanni
National Centre for Technology Management (Federal Ministry of Science and Technology), PMB 012, Obafemi Awolowo University, Ile-Ife, Nigeria
e-mail: abiodun.egbetokun@nacetem.gov.ng; omolayo.oluwatope@nacetem.gov.ng; david.adeyeye@nacetem.gov.ng; maruf.sanni@nacetem.gov.ng

© Springer Nature Switzerland AG 2019
G. Rexhepi et al. (eds.), *Open Innovation and Entrepreneurship*,
https://doi.org/10.1007/978-3-030-16912-1_5

Salter (2006) (henceforth LS). The broader and deeper a firm searches, the more innovative it tends to be, but search diversity[1] is subject to decreasing returns (de Leeuw et al. 2014; Oerlemans et al. 2013; Garriga et al. 2013; Duysters and Lokshin 2011; Jiang et al. 2010; Chiang and Hung 2010).

Our analyses are directed towards re-evaluating and extending the second empirical regularity described above. In this light, our specific objectives are two-fold. First, we explicitly replicate the analyses of LS, for the first time ever on a combined pooled cross-sectional sample of service and manufacturing firms from a developing country in Africa. For this purpose, we use a novel dataset on service and manufacturing firms in Nigeria, which is one of Africa's largest economies. The completely different sample and economic context help us to deliver additional insight to the strategic management literature on innovation and knowledge search behaviour beneath the frontier. Second, we extend the analyses of LS by taking a multidimensional view of innovation, and considering sectoral differences and the role of the economic context. In particular, we combine insight from the economics and management literatures to develop new hypotheses that link the firm's external search strategy to its sector of operation and the magnitude of innovation obstacles experienced. In the above respects, our analyses differ from and complement the recent replications of LS by Garriga et al. (2013) and Oluwatope et al. (2014).[2]

In the next section, we highlight the main concepts and results of LS, and draw attention to the specific issues that create the basis for our own analyses. After that, we describe our data, variables and some descriptive results before presenting the estimation technique and results. We discuss the results as well their implications for management theory and research in the final section.

---

[1] A clarification of terminology is essential at this point. Harrison and Klein (2007) make an extensive discussion of the diversity concept in the context of management research. Stirling (2007) presents a stylised framework of different aspects of diversity: variety ('how many types of thing do we have?'), balance ('how much of each type of thing do we have?') and disparity ('how different from each other are the types of thing that we have?'). Clearly, the notions of search breadth and depth used in Laursen and Salter (2006) reflect the aspect of variety. The term 'diversity' applied in other related research such as (de Leeuw et al. 2014; Oerlemans et al. 2013; Duysters and Lokshin 2011) actually reflects only the aspect of balance. Throughout this paper, we align ourselves with Stirling's broad framework and terminology.

[2] In fact, in (Oluwatope et al. 2014), the major objective was not to explicitly replicate LS. Hence, some of the LS variables were inevitably omitted.

Relating External Knowledge to Innovation: A Critical Discussion of Laursen and Salter (2006)

The existing literature is coherent on the positive benefits of alliances or external knowledge search for innovation. From a resource-based view of the firm, the so-called portfolio approach, whereby multiple sources are combined, is thought to be very useful (Faems et al. 2005; Jiang et al. 2010). The mechanism behind this hypothesis is the notion of diversity, which essentially implies different kinds of sources or partners. It is believed that diverse sources or partners tend to hold non-monotonous resources and are, therefore, better in combination than any single source. However, diversity has its limits. A smaller portfolio is easier to manage but holds less innovative potential. By contrast, a larger portfolio gives the firm access to diverse resources but is considerably more difficult to manage. Consequently, the relationship between firm-level innovation and diversity[3] of knowledge sources or alliance portfolio is curvilinear.

Perhaps the most influential study on this subject, to date, is the one by LS.[4] This is evidenced by the rapid diffusion of the breadth and depth concepts that the study popularised as well as the extensive forward citations (Fig. 1). In fact, as of April, 2014, LS has been cited more than 1700 on Google Scholar (an average of roughly 20 citations every month), more than 500 times in CrossRef and over 650 times in Scopus. Based on a sample of UK manufacturing firms, the study showed that using multiple external sources has an inverted U-shaped relationship with innovative performance. Their breadth and depth constructs, which reflect, respectively, the sheer number of external sources and the number of highly important ones, essentially capture the variety of external knowledge that the firm accesses. Comparing incremental (new-to-the-firm) and radical (new-to-the-world) innovations, they demonstrate that search breadth impacts more on the former while search depth impacts more on the latter. Chiang and Hung (2010), Garriga et al. (2013) and Oluwatope et al. (2014) document similar results for manufacturing firms in Taiwan, Switzerland and Nigeria respectively.

It is of note that LS is based on only the manufacturing sector in a developed country, UK. Thus, the external validity of the results and implications is debatable, particularly from the perspective of a developing country. This limitation is shared almost without exception, by later similar studies. For instance, the studies of Chiang and Hung (2010) and Oluwatope et al. (2014) are based only on the manufacturing sector; the (Garriga et al. 2013) paper replicates and extends LS by including a sample of service firms and considering the firm's contextual factors but is still limited in geographical scope. Moreover, to capture innovation performance, most studies in the LS tradition employ a measure of innovative sales, that is, the share of total sales that accrue from new-to-firm or new-to-market products. The narrow

---

[3]By this we encompass variety (breadth/depth), balance and disparity. See footnote 1.

[4]Garriga et al. (2013) recently noted that the analyses and results are highly significant for the research on innovation management and more specifically, open innovation.

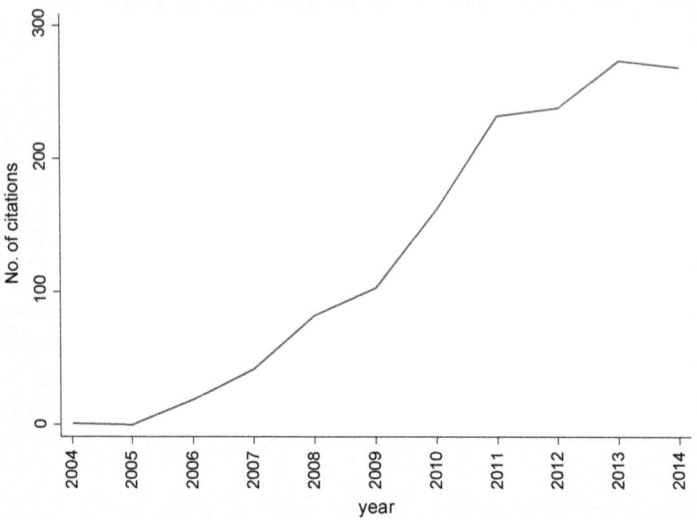

Fig. 1 Trend of Google Scholar citations to Laursen and Salter (2006) since it first appeared online in 2004. Note: Search string "OPEN FOR INNOVATION THE ROLE OF OPENNESS IN EXPLAINING INNOVATION PERFORMANCE AMONG UK MANUFACTURING FIRMS" ensures that the search returns articles that contain LS in the reference list. Search conducted on September 12, 2014 at 1 pm GMT + 1. The 2014 data is as at this date and the 2006 data was discounted by 1 to remove LS itself. In total, the plot includes 1422 articles

scope of this performance measure poses a problem for research in a less developed context. A focus on technological product innovation alone offers only partial insight on firm-level innovative performance. No doubt, firms make profit through the sale of their products, but the process, marketing and organisational capabilities that make production possible are just as important (Carvalho et al. 2013).

As Fig. 2 illustrates, the aspects of marketing and organisational innovation are especially important in a developing country. For our study context, Nigeria, and several EU countries, the figure compares the rate of technological product and process innovation (x-axes) in 2010 with the rate of non-technological marketing and organisational innovation (y-axes) in the same year. For clarity, we highlight only the study context and the EU average. In all cases, Nigeria is above the 45-degree line, suggesting that non-technological innovation occurs more frequently than technological innovation. The reverse is true for the EU countries, which are relatively more developed. Although this observation reflects the level of innovative capabilities in the latecomer firms, it is also strongly indicative of firms' innovation behaviour in the face of strong obstacles and in backward economic contexts (see Sect. 2.2 of Annex A in OECD 2005).

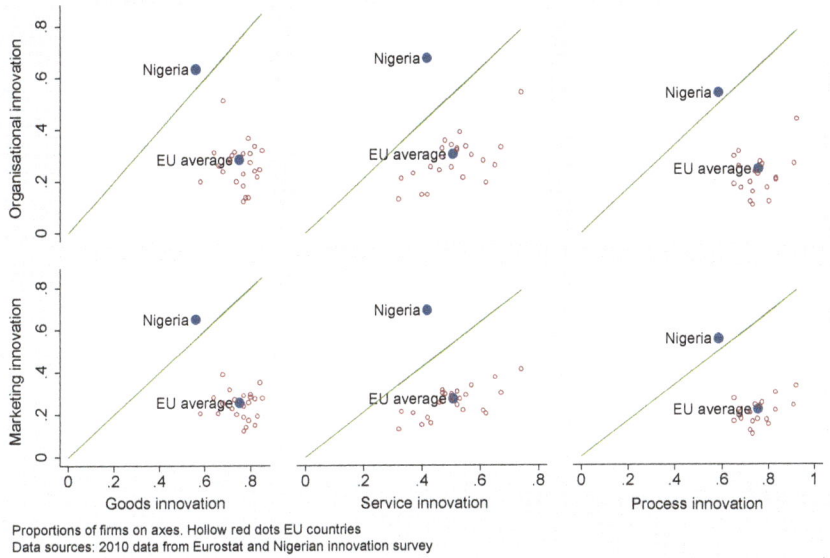

Proportions of firms on axes. Hollow red dots EU countries
Data sources: 2010 data from Eurostat and Nigerian innovation survey

Fig. 2 Organisational and marketing innovation versus goods, service and process innovation in Nigeria and the EU

Building Upon the Laursen and Salter (2006) Model

Considering the issues discussed above, a re-examination of the empirical regularity that LS championed becomes crucial, and we find opportunities for extensions in at least two main directions. We draw inspiration from three bodies of research: economics of innovation, open innovation, innovation management and development economics.

Sectoral Specificity

Studies on the economics and management of innovation have repeatedly argued that the innovation processes differ between manufacturing and services (Vega-Jurado et al. 2009; Castellacci 2008; Hoffman et al. 1998). Recent contributions to the open innovation literature echo this view (e.g., Garriga et al. 2013). However, in relation to external search for knowledge, the two broad sectors are thought to be very similar (Carvalho et al. 2013; de Jong and Marsili 2006; Archibugi 2001). For instance, based on Italian innovation survey data, (Evangelista 2000) highlighted the strong relevance of user-producer interactions in both manufacturing and services.

Nevertheless, given the nature of service activities, there are reasons to expect open innovation to work differently from manufacturing (Chesbrough 2011). For instance, the intangible nature of services implies that customers often cannot precisely stipulate their needs. Moreover, because the quality of services is hard to determine, suppliers are susceptible to a high risk of error and consumers often cannot provide reliable feedback. In addition, the non-storable nature of services often requires that producers, consumers and other actors in the value chain maintain doubly coincident schedules. More often than not, the offering of a service cannot be delayed and, therefore, any input, including knowledge, into the creation of the product must be available as and when needed. Thus, the "need to sustain a pattern of interaction over time, building up a shared understanding and common ways of working together" (LS, p. 136) is more intense for service firms. This difference will reflect in external search depth, leading to the following hypothesis:

Hypothesis 1: External search depth is more strongly related to innovative performance among service firms than manufacturing.

The Role of Economic Context

The context in which the firm is embedded affects both its innovativeness and external search strategies.[5] For instance, Garriga et al. (2013) showed that the abundance of innovation resources, especially knowledge, in the firm's environment tends to motivate external search. However, the environment in most developing countries is characterised by a wide range of obstacles to innovation, ranging from paucity of human capital and knowledge resources to poor infrastructure (Biggs and Shah 2006; Oyelaran-Oyeyinka 2006; Wignaraja 2002; Hadjimanolis 2000). The negative impact of these obstacles varies in intensity (Radwan and Pellegrini 2010). The variety in both the nature and intensity of the innovation obstacles affect the external search strategies of the firms in a unique manner.

Faced with diverse innovation obstacles, it becomes much more essential for the firms to search a wider technological or cognitive space. One way of doing this is to combine diverse sources in order to maximise potential external knowledge (Goedhuys 2007). This is particularly true given the fact that only limited resources are accruable from any single source. For instance, while customers may carry ideas for significant product improvements, they are of limited relevance in overcoming institutional or infrastructural constraints. However, industry associations are considerably helpful in making up for state failures and dealing with infrastructural constraints (Oyelaran-Oyeyinka 2007). Moreover, most firms do not perform in-house R&D (Ilori et al. 2000; Egbetokun et al. 2009) and inter-firm knowledge spillovers are thereby limited. In addition, the knowledge generating institutions like universities and research institutes often do not sufficiently create knowledge that is

---

[5]Interestingly, the latter aspect has not been extensively studied in developing countries. There have been a few studies of South African firms (Oerlemans et al. 2013; de Leeuw et al. 2014) but none of them accounts for the economic context.

relevant to the domestic private sector (Oyebisi et al. 1996). Thus, it seems reasonable to anticipate that as the range of innovation obstacles increases, particularly in a developing country context, firms feel the need to draw upon an increasing variety of external sources in order to minimise redundancy.

Moreover, as obstacles become more intense, it may seem logical for firms to repeatedly use the same sources that have been successful in the past. This partly explains why industry associations have become highly important in some sectors (Egbetokun et al. 2010, 2012). In addition, small firms, in the face of intense competition particularly from foreign imports and large enterprises, form repeated/persistent inter-firm linkages (or, co-opetition strategies, as they have come to be known) (Oyelaran-Oyeyinka 2005). The above discussion is combined in the following hypotheses:

Hypothesis 2a: A wider variety of innovation obstacles is associated with broader external search

Hypothesis 2b: A higher intensity of innovation obstacles is associated with deeper external search

Data, Measures and Descriptive Results

Data

The Nigerian innovation surveys are based on the Oslo Manual and, hence, share the core set of questions with the Community Innovation Surveys (CIS) of Europe. Hence, the datasets include information on the innovation investments, sources, obstacles and outcomes in the firms as well as detailed firm characteristics including size, human capital, age, location and export status. So far, there have been two surveys, both of which were inspired by the African Science, Technology and Innovation Indicators Initiative (ASTII). Some aggregate results from the second survey are reported in (AU-NEPAD 2014). The ASTII facilitated a process to make the Oslo Manual framework more relevant for Africa.

As already recognized in previous studies (e.g., Adeoti 2012), it is hard to plan a stratified sample in Nigeria due to non-availability of a consistent and reliable register of firms. Notwithstanding, the survey attempted a stratified sample based on the list of establishments with at least 10 employees obtained from the National Bureau of Statistics (NBS) and the Nigerian Stock Exchange. The Stock Exchange list includes only formal firms whereas the NBS list includes both formal and informal firms. These two sources were cross-referenced and any firm listed in both sources was automatically selected into the sample. The logic behind this is that if a firm was listed on the stock exchange then it must still be in the market. This criterion is important considering the fact that firm exit rate is particularly high in Nigeria, a factor that partly makes it difficult to compile a consistent register of all firms.

Table 1 Sectoral distribution of final sample

Year	Manufacturing	Services	Total
2007	521	207	728
2011	371	260	631
Total	892	467	1359

To ensure a fair geographical and sectoral distribution in the final sample, the population of firms was stratified into geographical zones and sectors (in the first wave ISIC Rev. 3.1 was used and in the second wave ISIC Rev. 4). The final sample (about 1500 in each round of the survey) was then selected based on proportional probability, with a combined response rate of approximately 45%. The survey instruments were delivered by hand to all the firms, and in many instances, some of the selected firms did no longer exist. In every possible case, the missing firm was substituted with another one in the same sector and geographical location. The two waves of the survey represent two repeated cross sections. Although it was ensured that every firm that responded in the first wave was contacted for the second wave, the response was particularly low, necessitating a re-sampling. Nonetheless, the amount of information contained in the datasets and their comparability with data from other countries make them very useful for rigorous empirical analyses. Table 1 gives a breakdown of our final sample, which includes a total of 1359 service and manufacturing enterprises.

Measures

Our main variables are fashioned as closely as possible after LS. Three different proxies capture innovative performance. The first two, INNMKT and INNFIRM reflect the proportion of the firm's revenue from new-to-market or new-to-firm products respectively. Our dataset does not include any information on new-to-the-world innovation, so we are restricted to INNMKT as the proxy for radical innovation and INNFIRM as proxy for incremental innovation. It has been repeatedly observed that developing country firms exhibit a higher propensity for incremental and non-technological innovation than their developed country counterparts (Ernst and Kim 2002; Mytelka 2000; Lall 1992; Oyelaran-Oyeyinka 2005; Oyelaran-Oyeyinka et al. 1996). To reflect this reality, we employ an alternative multidimensional measure of innovative performance that takes into account both technological and non-technological innovation. This third measure, SINNO (Cronbach's alpha = 0.66), is a categorical variable indicating the scope of the firm's innovative outcome, and ranges from zero (for a firm that carried out no innovation) to four (for a firm that implemented all of product, process, marketing and organisational innovations). Similar measures have been applied in previous studies like (Gronum et al. 2012), and it makes it possible to rank firms in terms of overall innovative outcome rather than by financial performance on only one aspect of innovation.[6]

Appendix 1 describes the usage of all nine external sources among the sampled firms. The variables BREADTH (Cronbach's alpha = 0.89) and DEPTH (Cronbach's alpha = 0.74) are constructed as in LS. They reflect, respectively, the number of external sources that a firm uses and the number of sources that are ranked as very important by the firm. To examine curvilinearity, we include the quadratic terms of search breadth (BREADTH2) and depth (DEPTH2). Firms were asked in the survey to rank on a scale of 1 (low) to 3 (high), the extent to which each of 13 factors hampered their innovation efforts. A factor not experienced was rated zero. Appendix 2 presents a summary of the innovation obstacles. The VARIETY OF OBSTACLES (Cronbach's alpha = 0.92) was constructed as a combination of these items, each item taking a value of 1 if the firm experienced it (low, medium or high) and zero otherwise. The INTENSITY OF OBSTACLES (Cronbach's alpha = 0.83) was constructed as a combination of the same factors, each coded as 1 if the firm ranked it high and zero otherwise. While the former reflects the number of innovation obstacles that a firm experienced, the latter includes only those that posed serious constraints to the firm.

To keep our specifications consistent with LS, we include dummies for whether a firm was founded within the preceding 3 years (STARTUP), has cooperation arrangements (COLLAB) and used customers as highly important source of information (USER). We also control for firm SIZE (the logarithm of total number of employees), and the major markets for the firm's products (GEOMARKT equals 1 for local, 2 for national and 3 for international). Contrary to LS, we proxy absorptive capacity by a measure of the quality of human capital (HUMAN CAPITAL) constructed as the ratio of employees with a university degree.[7] This better reflects the reality in the study context and is consistent with the research on the accumulation of capabilities in developing countries (Wignaraja 2002; Romijn 1997). The dummy variable SERVICE takes the value of 1 for service firms and 0 for manufacturing firms.

Descriptive Results

Descriptive statistics are given in Table 2. On average, 17.3% of the firms' revenue arises from new-to-market products and processes while 22.6% arises from products and processes that are new only to the firm. These figures are higher than those

---

[6]The values of this variable have purely ordinal meaning; higher scores correspond only to a higher innovation scope but not necessarily to a better financial performance. For instance, a firm with an SINNO score of 4 is not necessarily twice as innovative as one with a score of 2 but clearly demonstrates higher innovative capability.

[7]For this reason, our analysis excluded an evaluation of the Not Invented Here (NIH) syndrome which LS analysed.

Table 2 Descriptive statistics

Variable	No. of firms	Mean	S.D.	Median	Min	Max
INNMARKT	733	17.29	22.55	1	0	100
INNFIRM	734	22.56	24.54	20	0	100
SINNO	1359	2.39	1.36	2	0	4
BREADTH	1359	4.08	3.24	4	0	9
DEPTH	1359	1.64	1.91	1	0	9
VARIETY OF OBSTACLES	1359	8.26	4.35	9	0	13
INTENSITY OF OBSTACLES	1359	3.04	2.95	2	0	13
HUMAN CAPITAL	1025	0.24	0.27	0.15	0	1
USER	1190	0.17	0.38	0	0	1
SIZE	1341	3.86	1.33	3.58	2.08	9.74
STARTUP	1023	0.11	0.32	0	0	1
GEOMARKT	1359	1.47	0.78	1	0	3
COLLAB	1190	0.22	0.41	0	0	1
SERVICE	1359	0.35	0.48	0	0	3

reported by previous studies for firms in developed countries (for instance, LS for UK firms and Garriga et al. (2013) for Swiss firms). A possible source of this discrepancy is that both of our variables capture imitative innovation, that is, innovative changes that are not novel beyond the firm's primary markets but rather rely on basic science and technology developed elsewhere. This type of innovation is often implemented as a response to explicit market demand and is more likely to generate high returns in a large market like Nigeria. Table 2 further shows that on average, about two different types of innovation co-occur in the firms. This suggests that firm-level innovation is not a compartmentalised phenomenon but one that has a multidimensional attribute. As such, future research requires a multidimensional view of innovation to be able to study the process of innovation within firms more accurately. So far, the research is heavily tilted towards technological product and process innovation, which, though easier to measure through R&D and patents, offer only a partial picture of how firms innovate.

In our sample, search depth is less common than search breadth. Firms use about four sources of knowledge for innovation but they use only one source deeply, on average. Of all the innovation sources, customers, suppliers and competitors are by far the most important (Appendix 1), indicating a pattern similar to what has been emphasised in the previous literature (NACETEM 2010; Oyelaran-Oyeyinka 2005). Knowledge generating institutions like universities and research institutes are only weakly relevant to firms' innovation efforts. On average, firms experience up to eight different obstacles but only about three present major problems. These include infrastructural constraints and lack of funding both in-house and from external sources (Appendix 2). This is consistent with the earlier observations of (Radwan and Pellegrini 2010). Appendix 3 compares innovativeness, external search and innovation obstacles across the manufacturing and service sectors.[8] It can be observed from the table that innovativeness and search strategies are not substantially different across service and manufacturing but obstacles seem to be more varied and intense in the manufacturing sector. One observation is worth highlighting here, though. By definition, new-to-market innovation is far less common than new-to-firm innovation across both sectors. This, as already explained above, is connected to the business context. In general, due to knowledge, infrastructural and capability constraints, most developing country firms are better able to implement innovative changes new to them but not necessarily new to the domestic innovation system (Radwan and Pellegrini 2010; Mytelka 2000; Oyelaran-Oyeyinka et al. 1996). Notwithstanding, the fact that a non-negligible proportion of firms implemented new-to-market innovation suggests that innovation is not entirely beyond the reach of latecomer firms. Given that most of these firms do not perform R&D or secure patents, it will be instructive for future research to probe deeper into the sources of innovation in developing countries.

Estimation Procedure and Results

For all estimations involving the variables INNFIRM and INNMARKT, we applied a log-transformed Tobit specification as in LS. A Tobit specification is appropriate because the variables are double-censored. Specifically, we created a latent variable INN* for each of the dependent variables as follows: INN* = ln(1 + INN) where INN is either of INNFIRM or INNMARKT. The latent variable is then assumed to be a function of a firm's search strategies and a number of control variables including quality of human capital and market orientation. For estimations involving SINNO, we employed an ordinal logit specification given the rank-ordered nature of the variable. The purpose of this estimation is to examine whether a multidimensional view of innovation delivers results similar or opposed to the stylised LS results. Ordinal logit regression equations were estimated for BREADTH and DEPTH since they are also rank-ordered. With these equations, we present new results on how the economic context affects open innovation. Pairwise correlations among our variables are contained in Appendix 4.

The results of our attempt to replicate the canonical results of LS are given in Table 3. In general, our effect sizes in Models I and II are much smaller than those found by LS. For radical innovation, search breadth and depth are not statistically significant and the signs on the coefficients generally go in opposite directions to those found by LS (Model I). The coefficients of search breadth and depth are statistically significant only for incremental innovation. Moreover, the directions of the effects are similar to those found by LS only in the case of incremental

---

[8]Possibly because the time horizon is rather short, the main variables did not appear to vary significantly between 2007 and 2010. Hence, we do not emphasise time variation in our analyses.

Table 3 Explaining innovative performance among Nigerian firms by external search

Model	I (Tobit)		II (Tobit)		III (Ordinal logit)	
Dependent variables	INNMARKT		INNFIRM		SINNO	
Independent variables	Coefficient	S.E.	Coefficient	S.E.	Coefficient	S.E.
BREADTH	0.002	0.026	0.041*	0.023	0.709***	0.107
DEPTH	−0.003	0.024	0.068***	0.021	0.035	0.128
BREADTH2	0.001	0.002	−0.005**	0.002	−0.049***	0.010
DEPTH2	0.001	0.003	−0.005*	0.003	0.006	0.017
HUMAN CAPITAL	−0.123**	0.056	0.010	0.048	0.761**	0.307
USER	0.004	0.069	0.008	0.062	0.109	0.392
SIZE	0.026**	0.013	−0.029***	0.011	−0.072	0.062
STARTUP	0.011	0.052	0.039	0.044	0.133	0.219
GEOMARKT	0.033	0.022	0.029	0.019	−0.029	0.105
COLLAB	−0.013	0.065	−0.062	0.058	0.372	0.366
SERVICE	−0.169***	0.048	−0.008	0.039	−0.399**	0.193
No. of obs. uncensored	408		409		702	
No. of left-censored obs	196		150			
No. of right-censored obs	0		0			
Log likelihood	−171.57		−145.84		−823.28	
Chi-square	49.27***		45.55***		240.69***	
Pseudo R^2	0.126		0.135		0.128	

$*p < 0.10; **p < 0.05; ***p < 0.01$

innovation. We also find an inverted U-shaped relationship between search strategy and innovative performance only for incremental innovation (Model II). The corresponding turning point is four sources as against 11 sources reported by LS. Overall, our results on the relationship between search strategy and innovative performance partly confirm and partly oppose the findings of LS. LS showed that the effect of search breadth reduces as innovation becomes more radical, and our results go along with this. In the analyses of LS, the effect of search depth increases as innovation becomes more radical. However, in our analysis, search depth is more strongly associated with incremental innovation.

As is obvious from our data and methodological discussions above, the data generation process and the methods applied in this study are similar to those in the LS paper. This implies that one or both of the national context and cross-industry effects are responsible for the observed differences in results. Specifically, our sample is smaller and includes both manufacturing and service firms. Thus, smaller parameter effects and lower significance resulting from higher variance are to be expected. Moreover, as we have defined it, radical innovation is at the frontier of the firm's primary markets. It is worth noting that the primary markets in our sample are predominantly domestic—that is, local and national (see the descriptive statistics for the variable GEOMARKT in Table 3). As such, even though radical innovation could benefit significantly from external search beyond the national boundaries, the impact of searching within the domestic innovation system may be limited.

However, since incremental innovation represents a movement towards the frontier already defined by new-to-market innovations, it tends to be more responsive to external knowledge.

Our new multidimensional variable that captures the scope of innovation in a firm confirms the results for search breadth discussed above (Model III). In fact, the parameter effects are considerably larger than for both unidimensional variables and are more comparable to the effect sizes obtained by LS. However, search depth is not significantly associated with scope of innovation. In other words, a wider scope of innovation is strongly associated curvilinearly with broader search for knowledge within the domestic innovation system but not with deeper search. The turning point is about seven sources, suggesting that external search breadth starts to yield decreasing returns when the firm uses more than seven sources. Taken together with the corresponding turning point in the case of new-to-firm innovation, this result suggests that diminishing returns to external search sets in earlier in the Nigerian context than in the relatively more developed UK context.

In Table 3, the dummy variable SERVICE that sorts firms into service and manufacturing has a significant negative coefficient in the case of new-to-firm innovation as well as the scope of innovation. This indicates that on average, radical innovation and the overall scope of innovation are higher among manufacturing firms. Nonetheless, it says nothing about sectoral differences in the link between external search and innovative performance. This aspect is addressed in our Hypothesis 1which states that search depth is more strongly connected to innovative performance in the service sector. To examine this hypothesis, we included interaction terms, DEPTHxSERVICE alongside the dummy variable SERVICE. To balance the analyses, we add an interaction term also for search breadth. The results of the estimations are reported in Table 4. We find no support for this hypothesis as the parameter of DEPTHxSERVICE is significant only in the case of radical innovation, while the main effect of DEPTH is insignificant (Model IV).

We now turn to our analysis of the role of economic context in open innovation, the results of which are detailed in Table 5. On one hand, we have hypothesised that as the range of innovation obstacles experienced by the firm increases, the firm tends to search more broadly. On the other hand, we argue that as innovation obstacles become more intense, firms feel the need to search more deeply. These hypotheses find strong support in our sample. The parameter of VARIETY OF OBSTACLES has a positive and significant coefficient only in the case of search breadth (Model VII). As well, the parameter of INTENSITY OF OBSTACLES has a positive and significant coefficient only in the case of search depth (Model VIII). In alternative estimations (not reported due to space limitations), we checked for curvilinear effects by including the quadratic terms for variety and intensity of obstacles. No such effects were present in our sample. Quite interestingly, firms with better absorptive capacity—reflected in the quality of human capital—tend to search more broadly and deeply. The same is true for firms that have collaborative arrangements or treat their customers as a highly important source of information. The size of a firm as well as of its competition space (reflected in its primary markets) is significantly associated with search breadth but not depth.

Table 4 Explaining innovative performance among Nigerian firms by external search across the manufacturing and service sectors

Model	IV (Tobit)		V (Tobit)		VI (Ordinal logit)	
Dependent variables	INNMARKT		INNFIRM		SINNO	
Independent variables	Coefficient	S.E.	Coefficient	S.E.	Coefficient	S.E.
BREADTH	0.010	0.008	−0.001	0.007	0.228***	0.039
DEPTH	−0.001	0.021	0.030***	0.009	0.120*	0.062
BREADTHxSERVICE	−0.004	0.018	−0.006	0.014	0.101	0.066
DEPTHxSERVICE	0.052**	0.023	0.007	0.019	−0.088	0.121
HUMAN CAPITAL	−0.137**	0.055	−0.001	0.048	0.618**	0.301
USER	0.007	0.069	0.005	0.064	0.005	0.393
SIZE	0.026**	0.012	−0.034**	0.011	−0.082	0.062
STARTUP	0.022	0.044	0.057	0.045	0.137	0.221
GEOMARKT	0.035	0.022	0.027	0.019	−0.012	0.105
COLLAB	−0.013	0.064	−0.057	0.059	0.518	0.365
SERVICE	−0.284***	0.105	0.002	0.080	−0.785***	0.261
No. of obs.	408		409		702	
No. of left-censored obs	196		150			
No. of right-censored obs	0		0			
Log likelihood	−168.70		−152.28		−834.55	
Chi-square	55.01***		32.66***		218.13***	
Pseudo R^2	0.140		0.097		0.116	

$*p < 0.10; **p < 0.05; ***p < 0.01$

Table 5 Explaining external search strategies among Nigerian firms by innovation obstacles

Model	VII (Ordinal logit)		VIII (Ordinal logit)	
Dependent variables	BREADTH		DEPTH	
Independent variables	Coefficient	S.E.	Coefficient	S.E.
VARIETY OF OBSTACLES	0.043**	0.021	−0.021	0.021
INTENSITY OF OBSTACLES	−0.001	0.028	0.093**	0.031
HUMAN CAPITAL	0.470*	0.253	0.459*	0.268
USER	0.773**	0.337	0.855**	0.347
SIZE	0.121**	0.059	0.038	0.060
STARTUP	0.104	0.214	0.121	0.212
GEOMARKT	0.169*	0.098	0.115	0.101
COLLAB	0.716**	0.314	0.687**	0.321
SERVICE	−0.404**	0.187	−0.067	0.182
No. of obs.	702		702	
Log likelihood	−1504.34		−1189.48	
Chi-square	117.65***		91.24***	
Pseudo R^2	0.038		0.037	

$*p < 0.10; **p < 0.05; ***p < 0.01$

Discussion and Conclusion

This paper contributes to the existing literature regarding external knowledge search for innovation by manufacturing and service firms. Based on a dataset constructed from the Nigerian innovation surveys, we explicitly re-considered the LS model in a developing country context. On its own, this attribute of our study responds to a clear call in the prior literature for more studies that use CIS-type data from other national contexts, as a way to understand further, open innovation strategies and performance effects (Garriga et al. 2013). The results of the replication exercise are partially consistent with LS: both search breadth and depth are statistically significant for incremental new-to-firm innovation but not for the more radical new-to-market innovation. A possible explanation for this discrepancy, apart from the national context and the combined sample, has to do with the nature of the innovation process. By our definition, radical innovation occurs at the frontier of the domestic market since it is appearing for the first time. Such innovation is not likely to depend on an extensive search of the existing domestic technological space. In contrast, innovation that is new to the firm may benefit significantly from existing knowledge within the domestic innovation system because they lie below the technology frontier already defined by new-to-market innovations. Combining technological and non-technological innovation into a single measure, we find results similar to the existing literature only in the case of search breadth. We suspect that the observed difference stems from the inclusion of other types of innovation in addition to what is normally done in the literature. However, this argument is only tentative because we did not analyse non-technological innovation separately. Thus, further empirical evidence on how external search relates to non-technological innovation is needed. We believe that such evidence, together with what we already know about technological innovation, will help in building a more robust theory of open innovation, particularly with relevance for developing countries where non-technological innovation is of remarkable importance.

The results obtained from testing two new hypotheses deliver fresh insights on the relationship between a firm's external search strategy and its sector of operation, on the one hand, and the magnitude of innovation obstacles experienced, on the other hand. On these two aspects, the existing literature offers very limited insight. The aspect of obstacles is particularly important in developing countries as firms face diverse challenges in the innovation process. Firstly, we find that there is no discernible difference in the innovativeness and search approaches of firms across service and manufacturing. In fact, the link between innovative performance and external search varies only slightly between the two sectors. This is an interesting result given the recent rise of *servitisation*, whereby many manufacturing firms undertake product differentiation by bundling services with their products. The line between service and manufacturing has become blurred, and that is becoming apparent in the innovation and knowledge search process. Indeed, rather than support dissimilar firm-level strategies in service and manufacturing, our results suggest the absence of any strong differences in firms' open innovation behaviour and its link to innovative performance across the two sectors. Secondly, it seems that the economic context indeed influences the openness behaviour of firms. When firms face a wide range of obstacles, they feel the need to broaden their search horizon.

This stands to reason because, as the technological or cognitive space within which a firm searches expands, so does the amount of knowledge it can potentially access. However, in the face of more intense obstacles, searching broadly becomes less useful as it can lead to redundancy. Under such circumstances, it may be more beneficial for firms to use a few sources deeply, more likely those that have been successful in the past. Finally, absorptive capacity also plays a role in open innovation. We show that firms with high quality human capital are better able to scan the environment both broadly and deeply. Thus, we highlight, from the perspective of open innovation, the widely reported importance of human capital in the innovation process in developing countries (Wignaraja 2002; Romijn 1997).

Our results have further implications for management research and practice. For instance, it is instructive to note that, irrespective of sector, the type of innovation (radical or incremental) influences external search strategy. Nevertheless, this empirical observation begs further investigation. Future studies in different national contexts might confirm our results or uncover sectoral differences that we do not find in our sample. Furthermore, the point at which diminishing returns to external search for knowledge sets in is earlier in developing countries particularly in the case of new-to-firm innovation. This indicates that the domestic innovation system within which the firm is located affects both its innovativeness and external search strategies. Such effects may arise from variations in the abundance of external knowledge across national boundaries and, more importantly, from differences in the variety and intensity of innovation obstacles. In fact, as shown by Garriga et al. (2013), abundance of external knowledge positively affects firms' search strategies. Thus, future empirical works that are cognizant of the national context, particularly in developing countries, are needed. For future studies, it will also be of interest to apply datasets spanning a longer period. This should help provide answers to the issue of generalization and time. Finally, most firms operating in developing countries are in close proximity either due to being in clusters or some industrial districts. The effect of such agglomeration on search strategies should be of interest to policy particularly because it affects the abundance and flow of knowledge resources.

Appendices

Appendix 1: Sources of Information for Innovation Among Nigerian Firms, 2007 and 2010 Pooled Data (n = 1359)

Knowledge source	Percentage			
	Not used	Low	Medium	High
Customers	26.0	8.5	26.5	39.0
Suppliers	28.2	10.1	27.1	34.6
Competitors	34.4	15.5	25.2	24.9
Private laboratory	53.8	16.9	18.0	11.3

(continued)

Knowledge source	Percentage			
	Not used	Low	Medium	High
Universities	66.2	13.3	13.6	6.9
Research institutes	66.1	16.5	12.0	5.4
Conferences	46.0	15.8	24.3	13.9
Journals/trade publications	54.3	18.2	18.3	9.3
Industry association	40.6	15.4	26.1	17.9

Appendix 2: Innovation Obstacles Among Nigerian Firms, 2007 and 2010 Pooled Data (n = 1359)

Obstacles	Percentage			
	Not experienced	Low	Medium	High
Lack of in-house funds	25.6	12.6	19.7	42.2
Lack of external financing	31.2	14.3	16.9	37.7
High costs of innovation	29.4	14.1	20.6	35.9
Lack of qualified personnel	42.4	26.4	19.9	11.3
Lack of information on technology	36.7	28.6	21.0	13.6
Lack of market information	39.8	28.8	20.2	11.2
Difficulty in finding cooperation partners	41.1	23.3	19.4	16.3
Competition from dominant large enterprises	33.8	21.8	27.0	17.4
Uncertain demand	35.6	25.2	23.8	15.4
Poor basic infrastructure	23.3	7.6	10.7	58.4
Inadequate facilities	38.0	14.6	19.1	28.3
No need for innovation due to prior innovation	42.2	25.7	22.4	9.7
Lack of in-house funds	40.8	28.2	21.6	9.4

Appendix 3: Innovation, Search and Obstacles by Sector, 2007 and 2010 Pooled Data

Variable	Manufacturing (n = 890)	Service (n = 469)
Percent new-to-market innovators	15.6	13.0
Percent new-to-firm innovators	53.6	52.9
Average scope of innovation	2.3	2.5
Breadth mean	3.9	4.4
Depth mean	1.5	1.9
Average variety of obstacles	9.3	6.2
Average intensity of obstacles	3.7	1.7

Appendix 4: Pairwise Correlations Among Independent Variables

		1	2	3	4	5	6	7	8	9	10
1	BREADTH										
2	DEPTH	0.711*									
3	VARIETY OF OBSTACLES	0.022	−0.045								
4	INTENSITY OF OBSTACLES	−0.118*	−0.016	0.596*							
5	HUMAN CAPITAL	0.113*	0.135*	0.087*	−0.047						
6	USER	0.298*	0.307*	0.005	−0.036	0.113*					
7	SIZE	0.176*	0.118*	−0.093*	−0.196*	−0.040	0.095*				
8	STARTUP	−0.003	−0.033	0.004	−0.036	0.114*	−0.053	−0.123*			
9	GEOMARKET	0.187*	0.133*	−0.147*	−0.199*	−0.027	0.109*	0.290*	−0.047		
10	COLLAB	0.291*	0.288*	−0.036	−0.073*	0.103*	0.867*	0.138*	−0.091*	0.137*	
11	SERVICE	0.078*	0.107*	−0.336*	−0.327*	0.467*	0.010	−0.115*	0.122*	0.027	0.025

$*p < 0.05$

References

Adeoti, J. O. (2012). Technology-related factors as determinants of export potential of Nigerian manufacturing firms. *Structural Change and Economic Dynamics, 23*(4), 487–503.

Archibugi, D. (2001). Pavitt's taxanomy sixteen years on: A review article. *Economics of Innovation and New Technology, 10*(5), 415–425.

AU-NEPAD. (2014). *African innovation outlook II*. Pretoria: African Union–New Partnership for Africa's Development. Retrieved April 30, 2014, from http://www.nepad.org/system/files/AIO_2_Final%20Product[2].pdf

Biggs, T., & Shah, M. K. (2006). African SMES, networks, and manufacturing performance. *Journal of Banking & Finance, 30*(11), 3043–3066.

Carvalho, L., Costa, T., & Caiado, J. (2013). Determinants of innovation in a small open economy: A multidimensional perspective. *Journal of Business Economics and Management, 14*(3), 583–600.

Castellacci, F. (2008). Technological paradigms, regimes and trajectories: Manufacturing and service industries in a new taxonomy of sectoral patterns of innovation. *Research Policy, 37*, 978–994.

Chesbrough, H. W. (2003). The era of open innovation. *Sloan Management Review, Summer*, 35–41.

Chesbrough, H. (2011). Bringing open innovation to services. *MIT Sloan Management Review, 52*(2), 85–90.

Chiang, Y.-H., & Hung, K.-P. (2010). Exploring open search strategies and perceived innovation performance from the perspective of inter-organizational knowledge flows. *R&D Management, 40*(3), 292–299.

Cohen, W., & Levinthal, D. (1989). Innovation and learning: The two faces of R&D. *The Economic Journal, 99*(397), 569–596.

Cohen, W., & Levinthal, D. (1990). Absorptive capacity: A new perspective on learning and innovation. *Administrative Science Quarterly, 35*(1), 128–152.

de Jong, J., & Freel, M. (2010). Absorptive capacity and the reach of collaboration in high technology small firms. *Research Policy, 39*(1), 47–54.

de Jong, J. P., & Marsili, O. (2006). The fruit flies of innovations: A taxonomy of innovative small firms. *Research Policy, 35*(2), 213–229.

de Leeuw, T., Lokshin, B., & Duysters, G. (2014). Returns to alliance portfolio diversity: The relative effects of partner diversity on firm's innovative performance and productivity. *Journal of Business Research, 67*(9), 1839–1849.

Duysters, G., & Lokshin, B. (2011). Determinants of alliance portfolio complexity and its effect on innovative performance of companies. *Journal of Product Innovation Management, 28*(4), 570–585.

Egbetokun, A. A., Siyanbola, W., Sanni, M., Olamade, O., Adeniyi, A., & Irefin, I. (2009). What drives innovation? Inferences from an industry-wide survey in Nigeria. *International Journal of Technology Management, 45*(1/2), 123–140.

Egbetokun, A., Siyanbola, W., & Adeniyi, A. (2010). Learning to innovate in Nigeria's cable and wire manufacturing sub-sector: Inferences from a firm-level case study. *International Journal of Learning and Intellectual Capital, 7*(1), 55–74.

Egbetokun, A., Adeniyi, A., & Siyanbola, W. (2012). On the capability of SMEs to innovate: The cable and wire manufacturing sub-sector in Nigeria. *International Journal of Learning and Intellectual Capital, 9*(1/2), 64–85.

Enkel, E., Gassmann, O., & Chesbrough, H. (2009). Open R&D and open innovation: Exploring the phenomenon. *R&D Management, 39*(4), 311–316.

Ernst, D., & Kim, L. (2002). Global production networks, knowledge diffusion, and local capability formation. *Research Policy, 31*(8/9), 1417–1429.

Evangelista, R. (2000). Sectoral patterns of technological change in services. *Economics of Innovation and New Technology, 9*(3), 183–222.

Faems, D., Van Looy, B., & Debackere, K. (2005). Inter-organizational collaboration and innovation: Towards a portfolio approach. *Journal of Product Innovation Management, 22*(3), 238–250.

Garriga, H., von Krogh, G., & Spaeth, S. (2013). How constraints and knowledge impact open innovation. *Strategic Management Journal, 34*(9), 1134–1144.

Goedhuys, M. (2007). Learning, product innovation, and firm heterogeneity in developing countries; evidence from Tanzania. *Industrial and Corporate Change, 16*(2), 269–292.

Gronum, S., Verreynne, M.-L., & Kastelle, T. (2012). The role of networks in small and medium-sized enterprise innovation and firm performance. *Journal of Small Business Management, 50*(2), 257–282.

Hadjimanolis, A. (2000). An investigation of innovation antecedents in small firms in the context of a small developing country. *R&D Management, 30*(3), 235–246.

Harrison, D. A., & Klein, K. J. (2007). What's the difference? Diversity constructs as separation, variety, or disparity in organizations. *Academy of Management Review, 32*(4), 1199–1228.

Hoffman, K., Parejo, M., Bessant, J., & Perren, L. (1998). Small firms, R&D, technology and innovation in the UK: A literature review. *Technovation, 18*(1), 39–55.

Ilori, M., Oke, J., & Sanni, S. (2000). Management of new product development in selected food companies in Nigeria. *Technovation, 20*(6), 333–342.

Jiang, R. J., Tao, Q. T., & Santoro, M. D. (2010). Alliance portfolio diversity and firm performance. *Strategic Management Journal, 31*(10), 1136–1144.

Lall, S. (1992). Technological capabilities and industrialization. *World Development, 20*(2), 165–186.

Lane, P., & Lubatkin, M. (1998). Relative absorptive capacity and interorganizational learning. *Strategic Management Journal, 19*(5), 461–477.

Lane, P. J., Koka, B., & Pathak, S. (2002). A thematic analysis and critical assessment of absorptive capacity research. *Academy of Management Proceedings, 2002*, M1–M6.

Lane, P., Koka, B., & Pathak, S. (2006). The reification of absorptive capacity: A critical review and rejuvenation of the construct. *Academy of Management Review, 31*(4), 833–863.

Laursen, K., & Salter, A. (2006). Open for innovation: The role of openness in explaining innovation performance among UK manufacturing firms. *Strategic Management Journal, 27*(2), 131–150.

Lin, C., Wu, Y.-J., Chang, C., Wang, W., & Lee, C.-Y. (2012). The alliance innovation performance of R&D alliances: The absorptive capacity perspective. *Technovation, 32*(5), 282–292.

Lundvall, B.-Å. (1988). Innovation as an interactive process: From user-producer interaction to the national system of innovation. In G. Dosi, C. Freeman, R. Nelson, G. Silverberg, & L. Soete (Eds.), *Technical change and economic theory* (pp. 349–369). London: Pinter Publishers.

Mytelka, L. (2000). Local systems of innovation in a globalized world economy. *Industry and Innovation, 7*(1), 33–54.

NACETEM. (2010). *Assessment of innovation capability in the manufacturing sector in Nigeria* (Monograph Series No. 4). Ile-Ife: National Centre for Technology Management.

OECD. (2005). *Proposed guidelines for collecting and interpreting technological innovation data: Oslo manual* (3rd ed.). Paris: Organisation for Economic Cooperation and Development.

Oerlemans, L., Knoben, J., & Pretorius, M. (2013). Alliance portfolio diversity, radical and incremental innovation: The moderating role of technology management. *Technovation, 33*(6–7), 234–246.

Oluwatope, O. B., Adeyeye, A. D., Egbetokun, A. A., Sanni, M., Aremu, F. S., & Siyanbola, W. O. (2014). Knowledge sources and innovative performance: Evidence from Nigerian manufacturing firms. *International Journal of Business Innovation and Research, 10*(2/3), 209–224.

Oyebisi, T., Ilori, M., & Nassar, M. (1996). Industry-academic relations: An assessment of the linkages between a university and some enterprises in Nigeria. *Technovation, 16*(4), 203–209.

Oyelaran-Oyeyinka, B. (2005). Inter-firm collaboration and competitive pressures: SME footwear clusters in Nigeria. *International Journal of Technology and Globalisation, 1*(3/4), 343–360.

Oyelaran-Oyeyinka, B. (2006). Systems of innovation and underdevelopment: An institutional perspective. *Science, Technology and Society, 11*(2), 239–269.

Oyelaran-Oyeyinka, B. (2007). Learning in local systems and global linkages: The Otigba computer hardware cluster in Nigeria. In B. Oyelaran-Oyeyinka & D. McCormick (Eds.), *Industrial clusters and innovation systems in Africa*. Tokyo: United Nations University Press.

Oyelaran-Oyeyinka, B., Laditan, G., & Esubiyi, A. (1996). Industrial innovation in sub-Saharan Africa: The manufacturing sector in Nigeria. *Research Policy, 25*(7), 1081–1096.

Radwan, I., & Pellegrini, G. (2010). *Knowledge, productivity, and innovation in Nigeria* (Technical report). Washington, DC: World Bank. Retrieved April 30, 2010, from http://siteresources.worldbank.org/EDUCATION/Resources/278200-1099079877269/Knowledge_productivity_innovation_Nigeria.pdf

Romijn, H. (1997). Acquisition of technological capability in development: A quantitative case study of Pakistan's capital goods sector. *World Development, 25*(3), 359–377.

Stirling, A. (2007). A general framework for analysing diversity in science, technology and society. *Journal of the Royal Society Interface, 4*(15), 707–719.

Todorova, G., & Durisin, B. (2007). Absorptive capacity: Valuing a reconceptualization. *Academy of Management Review, 32*(3), 774–786.

Tomlinson, P. (2010). Co-operative ties and innovation: Some new evidence for UK manufacturing. *Research Policy, 39*(6), 762–775.

Vega-Jurado, J., Gutiérrez-Gracia, A., & de Lucio, I. F. (2009). Does external knowledge sourcing matter for innovation? Evidence from the Spanish manufacturing industry. *Industrial and Corporate Change, 18*(4), 634–670.

Wignaraja, G. (2002). Firm size, technological capabilities and market-oriented policies in Mauritius. *Oxford Development Studies, 30*(1), 87–104.

Zahra, S., & George, G. (2002). Absorptive capacity: A review, reconceptualization, and extension. *Academy of Management Review, 27*(2), 185–203.

Abiodun Egbetokun, currently heads the Science Policy and Innovation Studies department of Nigeria's National Centre for Technology Management (NACETEM). He holds a PhD in Economics of Innovation from Friedrich Schiller University, Jena, Germany. His research focuses on the sources and microeconomic effects of innovation and entrepreneurship. He recently coedited *Firm-level innovation in Africa: overcoming limits and constraints* (Routledge; 2018) and *Innovation Systems and Capabilities in Developing Regions: Concepts, Issues and Cases* (Gower; 2012).

Omolayo Oluwatope, is a researcher at the National Centre for Technology Management, OAU, Nigeria. Her educational background in social sciences as well as biostatistics has given her a broad base from which to approach many topics. She is a member of the team that executed the AU/NEPAD-funded African Innovation and Research & Design Surveys in Nigeria for two/three rounds. Her research and publication interests include science, technology and innovations management, R&D, developmental issues, and gender and reproductive health studies.

David Adeyeye is the Head, Planning, Programming and Linkages Department, National Centre for Technology Management, Nigeria, where his activities focus on planning, research, and capacity building on issues of science, technology, and innovation (STI) management. He is also the Desk Officer for the STI Indicators Project in Nigeria, the Nigerian component of the NEPAD's African Science, Technology and Innovation Indicators (ASTII) Initiative. Also, he is a doctoral candidate of Science and Technology Studies at the Centre for Research on Evaluation, Science and Technology (CREST), Stellenbosch University, South Africa. His interests are in innovation indicators, research performance, and innovation for inclusive development.

Maruf Sanni, currently heads the Technology Management Education and Training Department of the National Centre for Technology Management (NACETEM). He holds a PhD degree in Public Policy from the University of KwaZulu-Natal, Durban, South Africa. His research interests include low-carbon innovation development pathways and climate resilient development. He recently worked with the United Nations Development Programme as home-based intern and the United Nations University Institute for Natural Resources in Africa, Ghana, as a visiting scholar.

Open Innovation: Challenges of Integrating New Forms of Innovation in SMEs

Inga Haase

Abstract Open Innovation is a phenomenon widely researched in the context of large high-tech enterprises, but in recent years SMEs have shown a growing interest in engaging in open innovation activities. They have tremendous economic power, but each category (micro, small, medium-sized) is different and has its characteristics that need to be taken into account when planning to implement new forms of innovation activities. However, qualitative research on open innovation in micro, small or medium-sized enterprises is still scarce. Therefore this qualitative empirical case study addresses the question: How do small enterprises handle the process of integrating open innovation initiatives into the company?

The findings show there are three main areas essential for the integration of an open innovation initiative in small enterprises, all of which interact with each other: Communication, culture, and innovation. These areas led to the identification of four relevant, influential factors: Technical-operational management competence, operational-social management competence, social-technical management competence and the factor "words and deeds". The results confirm that existing approaches regarding open innovation in large mostly high-tech enterprises and SMEs do not fit the specifics of small enterprises. That means a differentiated assessment of open innovation activities is necessary and needed for different firm sizes. Based on these findings, the presented study offers a starting point for developing an appropriate approach regarding open innovation activities in the context of SMEs, especially small enterprises. The results provide new insights for theory as well as practice by making specific recommendations in relation to implementing and establishing open innovation in small enterprises.

I. Haase (✉)
Department of SME Management and Entrepreneurship, University of Siegen, Siegen, Germany
e-mail: inga.haase@uni-siegen.de

© Springer Nature Switzerland AG 2019
G. Rexhepi et al. (eds.), *Open Innovation and Entrepreneurship*,
https://doi.org/10.1007/978-3-030-16912-1_6

Introduction

Open Innovation in the broader sense combines internal and external ideas and allows for employees, customers, suppliers, cooperation partners, and even competitors to participate in different stages of the innovation process or initiate a project (Baldwin and von Hippel 2010; Chesbrough 2003; Chesbrough et al. 2006; Gassmann and Enkel 2004; Rosted 2005; Von Hippel 2005); it is the opposite of the closed internal research and development departments. In this study, I discuss open innovation based on the concept of producer innovators and single user innovators respectively a user-driven innovation approach (Baldwin and von Hippel 2010; Rosted 2005; Von Hippel 2005). This form of innovation goes one step further than the open innovation represented by the approach of Chesbrough (Chesbrough 2003; Chesbrough et al. 2006). Users should not only be integrated into some phases of the process but should also be able to actively approach companies and develop or implement innovation in all phases. Further, users are also demanding ever more significant involvement in the sense of prosumers (Kelly 2005) and pro-users (Bruns 2010). In this context, the term "user" does not only include classic end users or lead users but all those involved in open innovation processes (Kelly 2005). The literature mostly addresses, the different open innovation approaches in the context of large high-tech companies (Brunswicker and Chesbrough 2018; Chesbrough 2003; Chesbrough et al. 2006, 2014; Gassmann and Enkel 2004), but (low-tech) SMEs are opening up to this kind of innovation activity, too (Enkel et al. 2009; Gassmann et al. 2010). They are a driving force of economy as well as an important source of innovation (Muller et al. 2016, 2017). They are capable of radical (Acs and Audretsch 1987) as well as incremental innovations in their field of expertise (Abel 2006; Penzkofer 2005). Still, they focus on different areas and use different innovation models than larger firms (Acs and Audretsch 1990; Brunswicker and Vanhaverbeke 2015). The OECD (2002) notes, that SMEs provide comparatively fewer resources for innovation, and have fewer employees exclusively responsible for research and development activities. However, they overcome their lack of relevant resources through cooperation, for instance with suppliers (Van de Vrande et al. 2009). Regularly, these innovation activities happen in network-like structures to combine resources, distribute the risk among the innovation partners and to extend (technological) competencies and knowledge (Freel and Harrison 2006; Lee et al. 2010; Zeng et al. 2010). So, for SMEs cooperation with different partners or networks in order to innovate is a natural and typical process and although they have fewer resources to cope with the challenges of open innovation than large enterprises, SMEs (want to) use the advantages and opportunities arising from such innovation activities (Van de Vrande et al. 2009; Enkel and Gassmann 2010). Still, each kind of SME, micro, small or medium-sized enterprise has its characteristics. They differ from each other, e.g., regarding the structure and the availability of resources, and therefore they have different requirements and needs in relation to open innovation activities (Brunswicker and van de Vrande 2014). Nevertheless, in-depth qualitative research that focuses on the integration of open innovation in

SMEs is still scarce (Brunswicker and van de Vrande 2014; Gassmann et al. 2010; van de Vrande et al. 2010). Moreover, current research misses out on the differences between micro, small and medium-sized enterprises. Although, their specific characteristics, e.g., structure and availability of resources influence the needs in relation to open innovation activities (Brunswicker and van de Vrande 2014). Hence, this study addresses this gap by analyzing the integration of an open innovation initiative in a small enterprise in depth. For this purpose, I studied a small German enterprise from the construction industry over a period of 2 years.

The central research question of this study is: How does a small enterprise integrate an open innovation initiative into the company? In order to answer this question there is another aspect that I needed to address: why are they doing it that way, or more accurately what are the relevant areas, factors, and processes for integrating an open innovation approach in a small enterprise? This study uses a qualitative approach to answer the presented questions by conducting a single case study combined with an analysis based on the grounded theory (Strauss and Corbin 1996). A reflective, primarily inductive approach enriched by the use of deduction via state of the art literature (Goldkuhl and Cronholm 2010) is less susceptible to "desired results" and, as in this chapter, can show a research gap in the literature that can then be explored with a more open-minded approach (Strauss and Corbin 1996, 30ff.). Additionally, serendipity and abduction are a suitable complement to the research procedure mentioned above; diving into the field, letting the phenomenon take effect and adopting different perspectives. Based on this combined approach it is possible to make unexpected discoveries as well as collect various indications and clues about the actual phenomenon revealing new insights, topics or data sources. In this way, the study contributes new insights for open innovation theory and practice by identifying relevant areas and factors for open innovation activities in small enterprises and comparing the results with existing theoretical approaches and concepts regarding open innovation. With this, it is possible to provide empirical evidence about the different aspects that need to be addressed to meet the requirements, to take advantage of the arising opportunities, and to deal with the challenges of implementing an open innovation initiative, especially in the context of a small enterprise.

Open Innovation: Requirements, Opportunities, and Challenges

Companies that want to engage in open innovation activities need to meet specific requirements and framework conditions depending on their sector and pre-existing structures (Herzog 2011). These requirements and framework conditions include internal factors like the companies cultural development regarding the types of communication they use, the risk appetite of the owners or managers or how open and trusting there are. Other factors are the employee structure in terms of paths of communication or their hierarchy as well as the organizational structure in relation to the finances, or the number of qualified staff (Gassmann 2011; Herzog 2011; van de Vrande et al. 2010). External factors include market changes, competitors and customer requests that need to be addressed in a flexible way and depending on the situation (Gassmann and Wecht 2011). Another important aspect is a close connection between the internal project members (employees from different departments) and external innovation partners to ensure that everyone has the same information and is on track with the current state of the project. The heterogeneity of project groups or teams is also crucial to guaranty an extensive portfolio of perspectives and expertise (Bergmann 2010; Engel 2007; Gassmann et al. 2005). Regarding the opportunities of open innovation activities there are a lot of potential benefits like a broad pool of knowledge (Engel and Nippa 2007), a rise in customer satisfaction (Sandmeier et al. 2010) or the reduction of time to market and the costs of product introduction (Piller 2006).

Nevertheless, particular challenges and risks accompany these opportunities. These are for example related to the failure to adhere to the necessary requirements and framework conditions or rather an improper performance concerning the requirements and framework conditions (Enkel 2009; Hauschildt and Salomo 2011; Rahman and Ramos 2010). For instance a shortage of resources (Rahman and Ramos 2010) or adjustment processes regarding the needed cultural and structural changes (Piller 2003). These also include hurdles like not-wanting and not-knowing (Enkel 2009; Hauschildt and Salomo 2011); not-wanting describes the resistance within the enterprise based on disagreements or anxieties regarding the sharing of intellectual property, a potential outflow of knowledge or rather a loss of expertise (Enkel 2009; Gassmann et al. 2005). That reflects in the so-called not-sold-here syndrome; especially SMEs show an excessive amount of concern about possible outflows of potentially marketable ideas (Gassmann and Widenmayer 2010). Also, the enterprise has to implement new processes in addition to the daily business, and there are bureaucratic and administrative hurdles for example regarding intellectual property. Another factor is the classic not-invented-here syndrome; if external ideas or ideas from other departments do not stand a chance in the internal discussion, the best open innovation initiative is useless (Gassmann and Widenmayer 2010). The aspect of not-knowing refers to the shortcomings of the whole company regarding technical as well as administrative expertise concerning open innovation: managing previously unknown processes, dealing with new technologies, market requirements and partners or networks (Enkel 2009).

Further challenges are the selection, implementation and the handling of specific methods and instruments for the integration of cooperation partners in an open innovation project (Gassmann et al. 2005; Hofbauer et al. 2009) as well as the whole area of innovation communication (Bentele et al. 2004; Zerfaß and Ernst 2008; Zerfaß et al. 2004a, b). Innovation communication, in general, describes the internal and external communication in innovation processes with a focus on the internal and external process of interaction between the different stakeholders (Mast 2005; Zerfaß 2005b; Zerfaß and Ernst 2008); that affects the aspects of innovation management, corporate communication and also has an influence on the corporate culture. On the one hand, the internal innovation communication is used for employee communication to create a suitable corporate climate and to develop further and shape the corporate culture. On the other hand customer communication and public relations are used to promote the innovation, to increase the familiarity and gain the trust of consumers, journalists, and other stakeholders as well. It is the responsibility of the particular manager to get the target groups to understand and involve themselves with the innovation in a vivid and comprehensible way (Zerfaß and Huck 2007). That becomes evident in the context of innovation readiness (Zerfaß 2005a, b) Innovation communication acts as a catalyst for the innovativeness as well as for the innovative success (Zerfaß 2005b).

Additionally, most companies do not have coherent innovation strategies and structures to cope with these challenges resulting in difficulties regarding the joint planning and coordination of the project partners (Möslein and Neyer 2009). All these are factors that are relevant for implementing an open innovation initiative and are covered by existing approaches regarding large enterprises. The next section shows, how this study will address the questions concerning the particular needs and relevant factors for implementing an open innovation approach in a small enterprise.

Methodology

I designed this study as a qualitative empirical case study (Hartley 2004; Yin 2014) to address the research question. Case studies are a long established research instrument used in different disciplines; especially in the context of complex phenomena regarding individuals, groups, or organizations and social, political or similar research areas (Yin 2014). So, case studies make a significant contribution in terms of hypotheses and theory building (Eisenhardt 1989; Hartley 1994, 2004). Furthermore, the research question described in the introduction essentially relate to the problems of "how" and "why" (Yin 2014) and therefore require a flexible, in-depth examination and analysis in order to obtain a holistic picture of the events and to be able to derive action alternatives in the sense of the formed hypotheses and theories (Hartley 2004; Yin 2014). I selected the case because the company is a typical example of a small enterprise of the German Mittelstand. Data analysis is based on the grounded theory approach by Strauss and Corbin (1996) and Corbin and Strauss (2008) respectively. Grounded theory is used to analyze complex phenomenon's, characterized by social interaction especially in little-researched areas (Corbin and Strauss 2008); in this case, for example, the formal and informal communication and their influence, which are essential factors for open innovation activities. Furthermore, results gained with this method can be converted directly into specific recommendations (Corbin and Strauss 2008).

The findings of this study derived from the literature, an empirical analysis as well as a comparison of both. Current literature concerns the two research areas of open innovation and communication as well as their interrelations. For the empirical analysis, the study focusses on an example of the integration of an open innovation initiative in a small German industrial enterprise. The enterprise was founded in 1996 and currently has about 45 employees depending on the season, for it is a supplier of roof technology for the construction sector. There are two owner-managers, one is the technical management director the other is the administrative management director. Data comprises of five different sources: interviews, field notes, internal corporate documents, e-mails and media files such as images on the planning and integration of an open innovation initiative as well as the actual realization of open innovation projects (Corbin and Strauss 2008). Eight in-depth interviews with the two CEO's, employees, a co-developer, a customer as well as consultants of the enterprise were recorded and transcribed verbatim. They were conducted in German and took about 50 min on average. I translated all direct quotations from data into English. Purposive rather than random sampling was used to select respondents, who are well informed about issues related to the open innovation initiative and related processes. Additionally, phone interviews were conducted with two of the former respondents about 2 years after the initial interviews to get information about the development and the current state of the open innovation activities. Due to the wishes of the respondents, I did not record these but took notes parallel to the interviews. Altogether data collection covered 6 years, but the analysis focuses on a period of 2 years in which the enterprise tried to integrate an open innovation concept and to conduct first open innovation projects.

Data were organized and coded with qualitative data analysis software (MAXQDA), which helped to identify, explore, sort and edit concepts as well as categories in different stages of coding (open, axial, selective) (Corbin and Strauss 2008; Strauss and Corbin 1996). Figure 1 shows an overview of the research process and the different steps of analysis. The process is a circular procedure that I repeated until the analysis reached the point of saturation, and I had thoroughly explored the

Process	Analysis
Research question	Open Coding - Concepts
↓↑	↓
	Axial Coding
Theoretical sampling	- Categories
	Constant comparison
↓↑	↓
	Saturate categories
Collect data	- Main Categories
	↓
↓↑	Selective Coding
	Explore relationships
Coding	between categories
	- Core Category

Fig. 1 Grounded theory—process and analysis. Source: Based on Corbin and Strauss (2008)

relationships between categories. The first step of the analysis is open coding, searching the data for general topics, for so-called concepts which have specific properties and related dimensions. In this phase, the researchers familiarize themselves with the case and the phenomenon allowing patterns and ideas to emerge. In the next step, the axial coding concepts are getting compared, combined, clustered and connected in different and new ways; developing categories that subsume two or more concepts. More data is collected and analyzed to further build up the existing categories leading to a set of categories of which some are more developed than others. Some get eliminated because they are not as important as thought in the beginning or they are merged to form a new category. Data collection goes on as long as a point of saturation is reached; categories are well developed, and new data is not bringing new insights to the process. At this point, the researcher will be able to identify main categories. In the last step, the selective coding, the researcher selects one of these as a core category; the central aspect of the phenomenon which the other categories support and pivot around.

This approach allowed for a comprehensive analysis of the fundamental processes, interrelations and influential factors of an open innovation initiative. Thus, leading to an overall picture of the position of such an initiative in the company as well as its necessary connections with the underlying structures and processes. In this study, the main, as well as the core category, are characterized by two types of concepts: operational-descriptive as well as abstract-interpretative. Figure 2 shows the example of the category "Communication History" which highlights the importance of the analysis of the operational as well as the social level of the implementation of an open innovation initiative and the conduction of an open innovation project. Fully understanding the operational level is impossible without the social level. The category "Communication History" combines five different concepts that relate to expectations that new employees or cooperation partners like suppliers, customers or consultants are confronted with when working or innovating with the enterprise.

The first category that comprises of the concepts 1, 2 and 4 is "Great Expectations" because this is the overall motive of these concepts. In the companies self-

Communication History	
Open coding - concepts	Axial coding - categories
1. Welcome to the cooperative	Great Expectations
2. Guess the rules	
4. The way it always was	
3. Disillusionment	Appearance and Reality
5. Doing the job	
Expectations on the social level (green)	
Expectations on the operational level (blue)	

Fig. 2 Communication history. Source: Own figure

perception and the impression of new company members and cooperation partners the company is innovative, open and creative (concept 1). However, attached to this perception are certain expectations and behaviors that make it difficult for the involved actors to integrate themselves and to act by the cultural norms (concept 2). Moreover, the owner-managers have certain expectations regarding the rights and obligations of employees and external partners, which do not necessarily reflect the self-conception or the current situation and structure of the company and are not always communicated (concept 4). The analysis shows that there are two different types of concepts; concepts that focus on the social level and concepts that focus on the operational level. The findings show that the social level has a strong influence on the operational level; the self-perception (concept 1), as well as the informal rules of social interaction (concept 2), lead to expectations that directly address the way employees and managers are allowed to do their jobs. Overall the category "Great Expectations" is based on the perception that the owner-managers have of themselves and the company as well as on the underlying behavioral patterns of the owner-managers leading to specific social and operational expectations regarding employees, consultants, and other stakeholders:

Technical management director, p. 24	So, we need to hit the iron while it is hot, and then I can't look at the clock and say: "Oh, we have autumn, there is so much to do, so we don't know how to handle all the work, but I'm not allowed to exceed the 10 h today anyway."
Administrative management director, p. 35	The employee should not say: "Anyway, I will stick this in here, then it is done." But he has to say: "How can I solve the problem?" and when the problem is solved, we have to be able to produce it in piece production as well as in serial production
Technical management director, p. 25	Ok, we are working on ourselves, and we try to develop a certain understanding [for the employees]

The category "Appearance and Reality" addresses the perception of the described self-image as well as the related expectations and behavioral patterns. Thus, concept 3 describes the transition process of new employees, consultants or other stakeholders from the stage of early acquaintance to the stage of daily work-life; meaning from the reception of website content, promotional publications, guidelines and first conversations to the perception of the everyday interaction between the company members. Additionally, concept 5 refers to the familiarization with existing structures and processes as well as taking over the agreed upon tasks. On the social level, it becomes evident, that the perception of inconsistencies between the everyday interaction and the propagated conditions leads to negative effects for the person concerned (concept 3). Consequently, the social level influences the operational level; without identifying and addressing existing discrepancies, familiarization with structures and processes as well as the performance of the tasks assigned is not possible. Employees, consultants, and other stakeholders want to adhere to the agreed on arrangements and take over their respective tasks and positions; they will be "Doing their jobs" if the enterprise provides a suitable framework.

Results

In the case presented here, the enterprise tried to integrate an open innovation concept and the related structures and processes into the overall structure of the company. The open innovation concept used a coupled approach. They wanted to combine the ideas and knowledge of different partners (e.g., technicians, students, suppliers, layman) to develop products, services as well as processes beneficial for every partner involved. Therefore, the company must not only change its existing structures and processes, but it faces completely new challenges with regard to future interactions with diverse innovation partners. So, this study examined the integration of the open innovation initiative by comparing the theoretical basis presented above with practical processes, decisions and the behavior of the participants within the company. The used methodological approach allows for a broad spectrum of situations and behavioral patterns to be observed and supplemented by a variety of data. In this way, it is possible to carry out a comprehensive analysis and present fundamental processes, interactions and influencing factors connected to an Open Innovation-Initiative. These findings provide an overall picture of the status of such an initiative and the necessary interdependence within the company's structures and processes. The analysis has shown, that the categories and main categories that have proven to be relevant are characterized by the combination of abstract-interpretative and operational-descriptive concepts and the interaction of both kinds of categories. It resulted in the main categories "Influencing Factors of Culture Creation and Development", "Influencing Factors of Corporate Communication" and "Influencing Factors Innovation and Open Innovation". Based on these main categories and the related behavioral patterns of the different actors I identified three different corporate sectors as well as three different fields of competence that are essential in the process of implementing an open innovation initiative. These sectors are culture, communication, and innovation. The essential fields of competence are the social competence, operational competence, and the technical competence. As shown in the next sections, combined these sectors and competencies create an overall picture of the structures, processes, and interrelations that are the foundation of the implementation process of an open innovation initiative.

Culture, Communication and Open Innovation

The analysis of the different concepts, categories, and the particular relations provides explanations for daily behavior, issues, and discrepancies within the company; these became evident throughout the whole process of data collection and analysis. For instance the handling of innovation projects regarding product innovation in comparison with the handling of process or service innovations. Innovation management in product innovation projects was more developed and professional than the management in process or service innovation projects, for example regarding the adherence to deadlines and the different steps of the innovation process. These discrepancies became understandable after the analysis focused on the technical competence and the interplay of the related categories. It became apparent that the visible costs of a product innovation project are much higher than the visible cost of other innovation projects. These costs include raw materials, potentially new machines as well as the implementation and performance of marketing activities. With process or service innovations raw materials and machines are seldom needed. In these cases, the primary cost factor is the personnel deployment, but the owner-managers to not perceive personnel costs as additional costs. Because of resource limitations, the enterprise is not hiring any further staff; so, the existing staff has to conduct innovation projects in addition to the daily business. In this context, weaknesses regarding the areas of innovation, communication, and culture became evident. Working hours that employees and managers invest in innovation projects cannot be invested in the daily business, resulting in delays (delivery dates, processing orders) as well as monetary losses (missing out on discounts) and therefore inducing further costs. In combination with a general weakness regarding final implementations and the adherence to changes, this leads to never-finished projects and innovations that are, like the potential advantages, benefits or cost savings, not realized. On the social level, this behavior leads to a lack of under-standing among employees and cooperation partners as well as to a permanent restlessness and too ambiguous work processes.

Technical management director, p. 19 f	…it has just been the case that we were all tied up in our day-to-day business and we were unable to meet the deadlines constantly. Sometimes we would even just sit out the projects
Co-developer, p. 1	Projects are not completed, and before they have the chance to make a profit, they are rejected. Resources are used on things that are never implemented
Employee, p. 15 f	Because of the many projects [...] you feel like the hamster in the wheel, it is the same in other areas, because we just have to learn not to do too much at once, but that's what I think creates the frustration, the most of it anyway, up to and including being angry…

Another example is the companies' withdrawal into itself after the first steps of the implementation process.

Consultant 2, p. 14	No externals no [ideas from partners outside the company], I will tell you, we have regular service providers, like any other company, but no. Otherwise… Why? Hm, we do not care anyway

The enterprise has promising visions for the future, and the owner-managers, as well as the employees, are trying to comply with the relevant guidelines, but they lack perseverance. There are no good role models, crucial aspects and propagated intentions and behaviors are not sustainably anchored or lived by; this is true at the level of the owner-managers as well as at the level of other managers and employees. Eventually, all of them fall back into the old and historically grown structures. Thus, leading to frustration and a loss of trust between the particular parties and individuals involved in the implementation process or innovation projects. Furthermore, results show that the initial concept of the open innovation initiative did not fit the realization in the companies' everyday life; they use only those methods and instruments that solely rely on an outside-in approach. This situation can be traced back to the technical competencies, especially missing personnel and a lack of knowledge and ability concerning methods and instruments needed for a coupled process. Moreover, conducting this kind of process would have meant for the company to open up in terms of idea development but also regarding potential criticism which is traditionally hard to accept for the company.

Consultant 1, p. 7	Customers [...] said: It had to fail. The reasons for this were quite simple the executives in the company were basically not prepared to do this. To really open up and say: we want to do that, we let it happen and we are also open to criticism if it doesn't work properly
Technical management director, p. 29	I have to say the advisory board, in my opinion, has not achieved what it could have done. If one would have been ready [...] to allow real conflict situations to happen and to talk about different opinions there really but it has always been a relatively one-sided story with us

Besides most of the challenges, problems and risks mentioned in the first sections of this article are attributable to deficits regarding the social, operational and technical competence like missing resources (personnel), or a lack of competent support and adequate communication. The enterprise also has a high rate of fluctuation which connects with the social competencies and the behavioral patterns in the company. The perceptions, expectations as well as the behavior of the owner-managers and some employees, are not compatible in the long run leading to conflicts and ultimately result in employees voluntarily or involuntarily leaving the company.

Open Innovation: Integration

Based on the state of the art combined with the overall result of the analysis the findings show that there are three main areas important for the integration of an open innovation initiative in small enterprises: Communication, culture, and innovation (see Fig. 3). Each of these areas is crucial for the integration of an Open Innovation-Initiative, and they all interact with each other. The area communication addresses the operational level of corporate communication in the context of the planning, implementation, and realization of vital structures, strategies, and actions as well as the management of stakeholders and target groups. The area culture is limited to the social level of the open innovations cultural framework conditions and requirements. The area innovation includes the technical level of the innovation management; more precisely the planning and realization of innovations in the context of open innovation projects. Besides the supervision and the management of the individual areas, the enterprise needs special management competencies for the overlapping

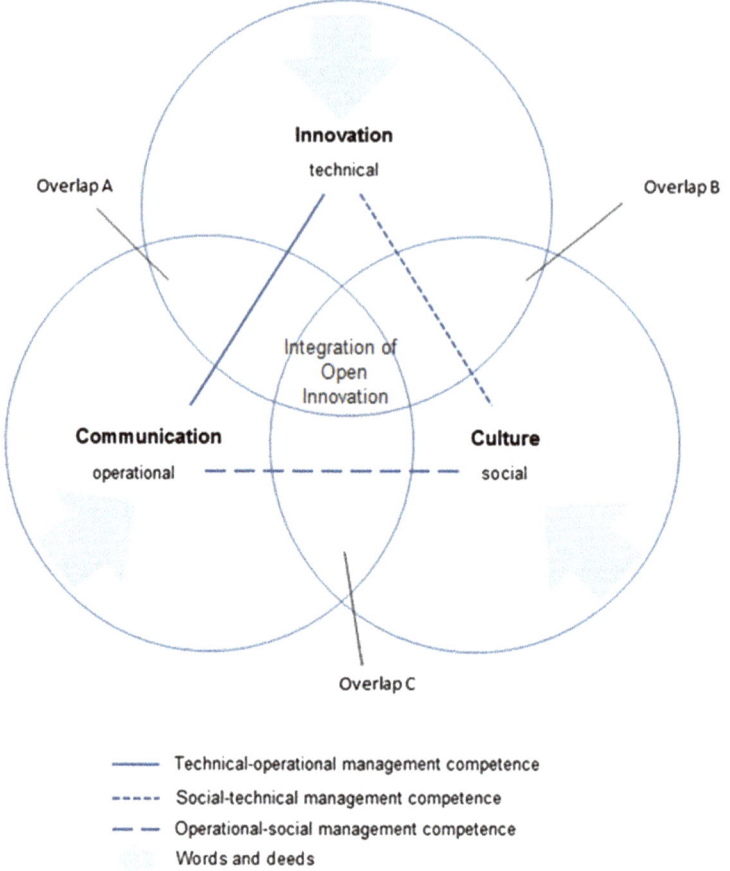

Fig. 3 Open innovation in a small enterprise. Source: Own figure

sections and the overall interaction between the different areas: The combination of these areas creates tensions the managers need to address in order to maintain equilibrium. In this regard, based on the fields of competence and the behavioral patterns mentioned above four relevant, influential factors have been identified: Technical-operational management competence, operational-social management competence, social-technical management competence and the factor 'Words and deeds'. The factor technical-operational management competence is concerning the interrelation of the areas communication and innovation as well as their joint responsibilities (overlap A). The factor addresses competencies regarding the innovation management, including the handling of the open innovation concept as well as addressing the individual perception the opinions and the concerns of the owner-managers, employees, consultants, and customers regarding the enterprise's open innovation activities and intentions. Moreover, it includes the support and coordination of innovation projects and project teams. Additionally, the responsibilities also include aspects of the external communication like contacting possible development partners as well as marketing and PR tasks. The social-technical management competence addresses the management of the interactions between innovation and culture as well as their mutual tasks (overlap B). Relevant here are the selection and the handling of open innovation methods as well as the organization and arrangement of development processes. Furthermore, tasks involve aspects regarding proper equipment like premises, personnel, working materials or the budget. The operational-social management competence relates to the interrelation of the areas communication and culture it describes competencies related to the cultural development of the company in terms of opening up the enterprise to internal and external ideas; meaning, the culture related interaction with the management, employees, consultants or other stakeholders. Moreover, the responsibilities also include the support of the members of the company, change management concerning cultural changes as well as the conception of strategies for internal communication (overlap C).

The factor 'Words and deeds' is an indirect factor and is based on the results regarding the behavior of the owner-managers and employees in the context of all three areas. The factor describes the discrepancy between words and deeds growing over time; attitudes, intentions or specific behaviors of the owner-managers and employees, not only in terms of open innovation projects but regarding the whole company are propagated via promotional publications, on their website, in conversations or on fairs but not lived up to consistently in daily business. Examples are the treatment of employees or customers, the handling of deadlines or the whole subject of corporate values like openness, reliability, honesty or respectability. Things like this can occur at the management level as well as at the level of the employees or stakeholders. This factor is of enormous importance for the conception and implementation of an open innovation initiative; nearly every aspect and area of a company is affected by the necessary adjustments and changes. If such discrepancies became visible or noticeable for internal and/or external stakeholders, it would have negative effects regarding the acceptance of the particular aspects like values, attitudes, behaviors, intentions, measures and the structures or processes concerned; possibly leading to an imbalance of the three areas communication, innovation and culture as well as to problems within the individual areas. Therefore, resulting in a failure of particular projects or the whole approach.

Discussion

The findings illustrate that the integration of an open innovation initiative, as well as the conduct of related measures and processes, poses several challenges for small businesses. In the beginning research on open innovation (Chesbrough 2003; Chesbrough et al. 2006) mostly ignored small (low-tech) enterprises, particularly the early stage of integrating such an approach into a company (Bogers et al. 2018; Chesbrough et al. 2014). Although the number of publications in this context is slowly rising (Usman et al. 2018), that is highly problematic because especially smaller enterprises with less experience and a higher risk, due to resource constraints, need suitable concepts, approaches, and competencies. In the case of the analyzed company, the integration of the open innovation initiative was not successful. Shortly after I completed data collection, the initiative has been shut down, and the enterprise has not reactivated it since. In the beginning, the company showed first approaches towards a cultural change and opened up to new structures and ways of cooperating with internal as well as external partners. Nevertheless, over time the commitment faded, cultural changes reversed and the company withdrew into itself ('Words and deeds'); proving the results of a study by Brunswicker and Vanhaverbeke (2015) who state that in a small enterprise certain organizational capabilities and managerial practices are needed to cope with openness and the integration of external knowledge. Additionally, the enterprise could not exploit most advantages and opportunities of the open innovation initiative (Piller 2006; Sandmeier et al. 2010). In this case, in contrast to the position adopted by the literature, most challenges and risks have not been preventable through structured planning or the knowledge and implementation of the requirements for open innovation (Enkel 2009; Sandmeier 2011). Furthermore, the scientific community has underestimated the impact and the central role of communication in the context of open innovation (Zerfaß 2009) as well as the interrelations and interactions between communication and the different areas of management relevant for open innovation. In line with my findings the concept of innovation communication (Zerfaß et al. 2004a; Zerfaß 2005b; Zerfaß and Huck 2007), although was developed in the context of large companies, addresses the three areas communication, culture and innovation management. Nevertheless, it does not cover the overall embeddedness of communication and the different levels and interrelations involved. Additionally, by focusing on innovation and the associated additional roles, tasks, and goals that go beyond the average level of internal and external communication, innovation communication requires the even greater use of resources than general corporate communication; a small company can hardly cope with these conditions. While they could handle some aspects and instruments, the existing structures and resources in most small enterprises would not cover the sheer mass of roles and responsibilities.

All in all, the findings show that a differentiated assessment of open innovation activities and their integration in a company is necessary and needed for different firm sizes (Brunswicker and van de Vrande 2014; Chesbrough et al. 2006). Based on the presented results, this study offers a starting point for developing an appropriate approach regarding the integration of open innovation activities, in the context of SMEs. Also, the current results are a hint for applying a more focused research lens when it comes to the analysis of a complex phenomenon like open innovation activities in SMEs; merely scaling down existing approaches for large companies is not an option (Turner et al. 2012). Moreover, I translated the findings into specific recommendations for action. In this study, a set of 20 strategic questions divided into the four categories strategy, resources, communication management as well as innovation and project management. These questions serve the company's initial strategic orientation with regard to future open innovation projects and can help small companies to identify and cope with potentially critical areas and challenges. This set includes questions such as: How must future projects be managed and what needs to change in existing processes? How many resources (money, time, personnel) can and should be invested in open innovation projects? Which actors and target groups are relevant to the internal and external communication of the respective project?

So, the results not only enrich and expand current research and scientific discussion but provide new insights for practitioners interested in implementing and establishing open innovation initiatives and conducting open innovation projects in small enterprises.

Limitations of the Study
The presented study uses a single case and while the company was analyzed over several years using various sources of data (Stake 1995) to minimize any bias regarding selective or expectation-dependent observations (Diekmann 2010) as well as hindsight bias on the part of the interviewees (Fletcher 2007) it is still only one case. Although, this study achieved analytical generalization by gaining detailed knowledge about processes, contexts, and behavior related to the analyzed phenomenon and thus can identify and transfer relevant conditions and patterns (Hartley 2004; Strauss and Corbin 1996; Yin 2014), the transferability is limited.

As mentioned in the methodology section the selected case is a small industrial enterprise with one production site and capital-intensive machinery. There are specific structures and framework conditions that need to be met by the company to operate successfully on the market: for example the dependence on suppliers of raw materials or specific machines. Therefore, the transferability to other sectors with potentially different structures and framework conditions is not guaranteed or rather it needs further exploration. Hence, the next step should be a longitudinal study with a large sample to test and validate the results of this initial basic research.

Conclusion

This study contributes novel insights into the areas and factors relevant for implementing an open innovation initiative as well as the respective interrelations and their embeddedness in the overall structure of a company. The results show that proper management of the identified fields of competence is needed to create the framework conditions and meet the requirements that are essential for the implementation and the long-term success of an open innovation concept in a small enterprise.

Furthermore, the findings confirm that existing approaches regarding open innovation in large mostly high-tech enterprises as well as small and medium-sized enterprises, seen as one major group, do not logically fit the specific contexts, characteristics, and needs of small enterprises. Some aspects of open innovation approaches like possible methods and instruments are flexible enough to be used in the context of small enterprises, and there is some research in this respect (Brunswicker and van de Vrande 2014; Rahman and Ramos 2010; Van de Vrande et al. 2009). Nevertheless, the overall concepts combined with the findings of this study illustrate a lack of applicability. The same is true with regard to the innovation communication theories. It is evident that the field needs more research regarding the actual integration of open innovation initiatives into small and medium-sized enterprises as well as the corresponding structures and processes.

References

Abel, R. (2006). Innovationen in Kleinunternehmen: Wahrnehmung, Wirklichkeit und Wege. In R. Abel, H. H. Bass, & R. Ernst-Siebert (Eds.), *Kleine und mittelgroße Unternehmen im globalen Innovationswettbewerb: Technikgestaltung, Internationalisierungsstrategien, Beschäftigungsschaffung* (1st ed., pp. 63–87). München: Hampp.

Acs, Z. J., & Audretsch, D. B. (1987). Innovation in large and small firms. *Economics Letters, 23* (1), 109–112.

Acs, Z. J., & Audretsch, D. B. (1990). *Innovation and small firms* (2. printing). Cambridge, MA: MIT Press.

Baldwin, C. Y., & von Hippel, E. A. (2010). *Modeling a paradigm shift: From producer innovation to user and open collaborative innovation* (No. 10-038). Retrieved from http://poseidon01.ssrn. com/delivery.php?ID=073073021078082081094120081112090024051051004040033087102079009075003124093004122090054018020099090803206202509111108900210901905700109501407706412506610912300702601800308800610606809209402807808411510302810102501502207210600812512510809208109200 3&EXT=pdf

Bentele, G., Piwinger, M., & Schönborn, G. (Eds.). (2004). *Innovationskommunikation – Strategisches Handlungsfeld für Corporate Communications. Kommunikationsmanagement (Loseblattwerk 2001 ff.): Vol. 124.* Neuwied: Luchterhand.

Bergmann, G. (2010). *Erfinderische Ökonomie. Essay, Köln/Siegen.* Retrieved from http://www. wiwi.uni-siegen.de/inno/download/pdf_dateien/erf_oekongbneu%5B1%5D.pdf

Bogers, M., Chesbrough, H., & Moedas, C. (2018). Open innovation: Research, practices, and policies. *California Management Review, 60*(2), 5–16. https://doi.org/10.1177/00081256 17745086.

Bruns, A. (2010). Vom Prosumenten zum Produtzer. In B. Blättel-Mink & K.-U. Hellmann (Eds.), *Konsumsoziologie und Massenkultur. Prosumer Revisited: Zur Aktualität einer Debatte* (1st ed., pp. 191–205). Wiesbaden: VS Verl. für Sozialwiss.

Brunswicker, S., & Chesbrough, H. (2018). The adoption of open innovation in large firms. *Research-Technology Management, 61*(1), 35–45. https://doi.org/10.1080/08956308.2018. 1399022.

Brunswicker, S., & van de Vrande, V. (2014). Exploring open innovation in small and medium-sized enterprises. In H. Chesbrough, W. van Haverbeke, & J. West (Eds.), *New frontiers in open innovation* (1st ed., pp. 135–156). Oxford: Oxford Univ. Press.

Brunswicker, S., & Vanhaverbeke, W. (2015). Open innovation in small and medium-sized enterprises (SMEs): External knowledge sourcing strategies and internal organizational facilitators. *Journal of Small Business Management, 53*(4), 1241–1263. https://doi.org/10.1111/ jsbm.12120.

Chesbrough, H. W. (2003). *Open innovation: The new imperative for creating and profiting from technology.* Boston, MA: Harvard Business School Press.

Chesbrough, H. W., Vanhaverbeke, W., & West, J. (Eds.). (2006). *Open innovation: Researching a new paradigm.* Oxford: Oxford Univ. Press.

Chesbrough, H., van Haverbeke, W., & West, J. (Eds.). (2014). *New frontiers in open innovation* (1st ed.). Oxford: Oxford Univ. Press.

Corbin, J. M., & Strauss, A. L. (2008). *Basics of qualitative research: Techniques and procedures for developing grounded theory* (3rd ed.). Los Angeles, CA: Sage.

Diekmann, A. (2010). Empirische Sozialforschung: Grundlagen, Methoden, Anwendungen. In *Rororo Rowohlts Enzyklopädie* (4 Aufl.). Reinbek bei Hamburg: Rowohlt-Taschenbuch-Verl.

Eisenhardt, K. M. (1989). Building theories from case study research. *Academy of Management Review, 14*(4), 532–550. Retrieved from http://www.jstor.org/stable/258557?seq=2

Engel, K. (2007). Organisation von Innovationsmanagement. In K. Engel & M. Nippa (Eds.), *Innovationsmanagement: Von der Idee zum erfolgreichen Produkt* (pp. 1–14). Heidelberg: Physica-Verl.

Engel, K., & Nippa, M. (Eds.). (2007). *Innovationsmanagement: Von der Idee zum erfolgreichen Produkt*. Heidelberg: Physica-Verl. Retrieved from http://hsu-hh.ciando.com/shop/book/short/index.cfm/fuseaction/short/bok_id/12675

Enkel, E. (2009). Chancen und Risiken von Open Innovation. In A. Zerfaß & K. M. Möslein (Eds.), *Kommunikation als Erfolgsfaktor im Innovationsmanagement* (pp. 177–192). Wiesbaden: Gabler.

Enkel, E., & Gassmann, O. (2010). Creative imitation: Exploring the case of cross-industry innovation. *R&D Management, 40*(3), 256–270. Retrieved from http://onlinelibrary.wiley.com/doi/10.1111/j.1467-9310.2010.00591.x/full

Enkel, E., Gassmann, O., & Chesbrough, H. (2009). Open R&D and open innovation: Exploring the phenomenon. *R&D Management, 39*(4), 311–316.

Fletcher, D. (2007). 'Toy story': The narrative world of entrepreneurship and the creation of interpretive communities. *Journal of Business Venturing, 22*(5), 649–672.

Freel, M. S., & Harrison, R. T. (2006). Innovation and cooperation in the small firm sector: Evidence from 'Northern Britain'. *Regional Studies, 40*(4), 289–305. https://doi.org/10.1080/00343400600725095.

Gassmann, O. (2011). Innovation: Zufall oder Management? In O. Gassmann & P. Sutter (Eds.), *Praxiswissen Innovationsmanagement: Von der Idee zum Markterfolg* (2nd ed., pp. 1–26). München: Hanser.

Gassmann, O., & Enkel, E. (2004). Towards a theory of open innovation: Three core process archetypes. In *R&D management conference* (Vol. 6, pp. 1–18). Retrieved from http://www.alexandria.unisg.ch/publications/274

Gassmann, O., & Wecht, C. H. (2011). Technologiestrategie: Von der Vision zur Aktion. In O. Gassmann & P. Sutter (Eds.), *Praxiswissen Innovationsmanagement: Von der Idee zum Markterfolg* (2nd ed., pp. 27–39). München: Hanser.

Gassmann, O., & Widenmayer, B. (2010). Open Innovation: Vom Schlagwort zum praktischen Tool. *Technische Rundschau, 2*, 56–57. Retrieved from https://www.alexandria.unisg.ch/Publications/citation/Oliver_Gassmann/60033/DESC-type

Gassmann, O., Kausch, C., & Enkel, E. (2005). Einbeziehung des Kunden in einer frühen Phase des Innovationsprozesses. *Thexis, 22*(2), 9–12. (S. 1–9). Retrieved from http://www.alexandria.unisg.ch/publications/8569

Gassmann, O., Enkel, E., & Chesbrough, H. (2010). The future of open innovation. *R&D Management, 40*(3), 213–221. Retrieved from http://onlinelibrary.wiley.com/doi/10.1111/j.1467-9310.2010.00605.x/pdf

Goldkuhl, G., & Cronholm, S. (2010). Adding theoretical grounding to grounded theory: Toward multi-grounded theory. *International Journal of Qualitative Methods, 9*(2), 187–205.

Hartley, J. F. (1994). Case studies in organizational research. In C. Cassell & G. Symon (Eds.), *Qualitative methods in organizational research: A practical guide* (pp. 208–229). London: Sage.

Hartley, J. F. (2004). Case study research. In C. Cassell (Ed.), *Essential guide to qualitative methods in organizational research* (pp. 323–333). London: Sage.

Hauschildt, J., & Salomo, S. (2011). Innovationsmanagement. In *Vahlens Handbücher der Wirtschafts- und Sozialwissenschaften* (5., überarb., erg. und aktual. Aufl.). München: Vahlen. Retrieved from http://site.ebrary.com/lib/alltitles/docDetail.action?docID=10602052

Herzog, P. (2011). Open and closed innovation. In *Betriebswirtschaftliche Studien in forschungsintensiven Industrien*. Wiesbaden: Springer Fachmedien. Retrieved from http://gbv.eblib.com/patron/FullRecord.aspx?p=749176

Hofbauer, G., Körner, R., Nikolaus, U., & Poost, A. (2009). *Marketing von Innovationen: Strategien und Mechanismen zur Durchsetzung von Innovationen*. Stuttgart: Kohlhammer. Retrieved from http://deposit.d-nb.de/cgi-bin/dokserv?id=3111368&prov=M&dok_var=1&dok_ext=htm

Kelly, K. (2005). We are the web. *Wired Magazine, 13*(8), 113–123.

Lee, S., Park, G., Yoon, B., & Park, J. (2010). Open innovation in SMEs—An intermediated network model. *Research Policy, 39*(2), 290–300. https://doi.org/10.1016/j.respol.2009.12.009.

Mast, C. (2005). Innovation als Herausforderung für die Unternehmenskommunikation. In C. Mast & A. Zerfaß (Eds.), *Neue Ideen erfolgreich durchsetzen. Das Handbuch der Innovationskommunikation* (pp. 43–57). Frankfurt a. M: Frankfurter Allgemeine Buch.

Möslein, K. M., & Neyer, A.-K. (2009). Open Innovation. - Grundlagen, Herausforderungen, Spannungsfelder. In A. Zerfaß & K. M. Möslein (Hg.), *Kommunikation als Erfolgsfaktor im Innovationsmanagement* (pp. 85–103). Wiesbaden: Gabler.

Muller, P., Devnani, S., Julius, J., Gagliardi, D., & Marzocchi, C. (2016). *Annual report on European SMEs: 2015/2016*. Retrieved from European Union website https://ec.europa.eu/jrc/sites/jrcsh/files/annual_report_-_eu_smes_2015-16.pdf

Muller, P., Julius, J., Herr, D., Koch, L., Peycheva, V., & McKiernan, S. (2017). *Annual report on European SMEs: 2016/2017*. Retrieved from European Union website https://ec.europa.eu/growth/smes/business-friendly-environment/performance-review_en

OECD. (2002). *Frascati manual 2002: The measurement of scientific and technological activities; proposed standard practice for surveys of research and experimental development* (6th ed.). Paris: OECD.

Penzkofer, H. (2005). Anstieg der Industrieinnovationen setzte sich 2004 fort. *ifo Schnelldienst, 58*(5), 42–49. Retrieved from https://EconPapers.repec.org/RePEc:ces:ifosdt:v:58:y:2005:i:05:p:42-49

Piller, F. (2003). Von open source zu open innovation. *Harvard Business Manager, 25*(12), 114.

Piller, F. T. (2006). User innovation: Der Kunde kann's besser. In O. Drossou, S. Krempl, & A. Poltermann (Eds.), *Telepolis. Die wunderbare Wissensvermehrung: Wie Open Innovation unsere Welt revolutioniert* (1st ed., pp. 85–97). Hannover: Heise. Retrieved from http://www.downloads.mass-customization.de/pil2005-1.pdf

Rahman, H., & Ramos, I. (2010). Open innovation in SMEs: From closed boundaries to networked paradigm. *Issues in Informing Science and Information Technology, 7*, 471–487. Retrieved from http://iisit.org/Vol7/IISITv7p471-487Rahman792.pdf

Rosted, J. (2005). *User-driven innovation: Results and recommendations*. Copenhagen: FORA. Retrieved from http://www.euc2c.com/graphics/en/pdfs/mod3/userdriveninnovation.pdf

Sandmeier, P. (2011). Der Kunde als Innovationsmotor. In O. Gassmann & P. Sutter (Eds.), *Praxiswissen Innovationsmanagement: Von der Idee zum Markterfolg* (2nd ed., pp. 127–144). München: Hanser.

Sandmeier, P., Morrison, P. D., & Gassmann, O. (2010). Integrating customers in product innovation: Lessons from industrial development contractors and in-house contractors in rapidly changing customer markets. *Creativity and Innovation Management, 19*(2), 89–106. Retrieved from. Retrieved from http://onlinelibrary.wiley.com/doi/10.1111/j.1467-8691.2010.00555.x/abstract;jsessionid=A6B6F47CBA3DE24D50EFCAB8C06F0CF9.d04t03?

Stake, R. E. (1995). *The art of case study research*. Thousand Oaks, CA: Sage.

Strauss, A., & Corbin, J. (1996). *Grounded theory: Grundlagen qualitativer Sozialforschung*. Weinheim: Beltz.

Turner, R. J., Ledwith, A., & Kelly, J. (2012). Project management in small to medium-sized enterprises: Tailoring the practices to the size of company. *Management Decision, 50*(5), 942–957. https://doi.org/10.1108/00251741211227627.

Usman, M., Roijakkers, N., Vanhaverbeke, W., & Frattini, F. (2018). A systematic review of the literature on open innovation in SMEs. In W. Vanhaverbeke, F. Frattini, N. Roijakkers, & M. Usman (Eds.), *Researching open innovation in SMEs* (pp. 3–35). Hackensack, NJ: World Scientific.

Van de Vrande, V., de Jong, J. P. J., Vanhaverbeke, W., & de Rochemont, M. (2009). Open innovation in SMEs: Trends, motives and management challenges. *Technovation, 29*(6), 423–437. Retrieved from http://www.sciencedirect.com/science/article/pii/S0166497208001314

Van de Vrande, V., Vanhaverbeke, W., & Gassmann, O. (2010). Broadening the scope of open innovation: Past research, current state and future directions. *International Journal of Technology Management, 52*(3/4), 221–235.

Von Hippel, E. (2005). *Democratizing innovation.* Cambridge: The MIT Press. Retrieved from http://web.mit.edu/evhippel/www/democ1.htm

Yin, R. K. (2014). *Case study research: Design and methods* (5th ed.). Los Angeles, CA: Sage.

Zeng, S. X., Xie, X. M., & Tam, C. M. (2010). Relationship between cooperation networks and innovation performance of SMEs. *Technovation, 30*(3), 181–194. https://doi.org/10.1016/j.technovation.2009.08.003.

Zerfaß, A. (2005a). Innovation readiness. *Innovation Journalism, 2*(8), 1–27. Retrieved from http://168.144.24.220/archive/INJO-2-4_split/INJO-2-4%20pp.229-255.pdf

Zerfaß, A. (2005b). Innovationsmanagement und Innovationskommunikation: Erfolgsfaktor für Unternehmen und Region. In C. Mast & A. Zerfaß (Eds.), *Neue Ideen erfolgreich durchsetzen. Das Handbuch der Innovationskommunikation* (pp. 16–42). Frankfurt a. M: Frankfurter Allgemeine Buch.

Zerfaß, A. (2009). Kommunikation als konstitutives Element im Innovationsmanagement: Soziologische und kommunikationswissenschaftliche Grundlagen der Open Innovation. In A. Zerfaß & K. M. Möslein (Eds.), *Kommunikation als Erfolgsfaktor im Innovationsmanagement* (pp. 23–55). Wiesbaden: Gabler. https://doi.org/10.1007/978-3-8349-8242-1_2.

Zerfaß, A., & Ernst, N. (2008). *Kommunikation als Erfolgsfaktor im Innovationsmanagement: Ergebnisse einer Studie in deutschen Zukunftstechnologie-Branchen.* Retrieved from https://www.ffpr.de/wp-content/uploads/2012/05/Ergebnisbericht_Studie_Kommunikation_Innovationsmanagement_-_Uni_Leipzig_-_April_2008-1.pdf

Zerfaß, A., & Huck, S. (2007). Innovationskommunikation: Neue Produkte, Ideen und Technologien erfolgreich positionieren. In M. Piwinger & A. Zerfaß (Eds.), *Handbuch Unternehmenskommunikation* (1st ed., pp. 847–858). Wiesbaden: Gabler Verlag/Springer Fachmedien Wiesbaden GmbH.

Zerfaß, A., Sandhu, S., & Huck, S. (2004a). Innovationskommunikation – Strategisches Handlungsfeld für Corporate Communications. In G. Bentele, M. Piwinger, & G. Schönborn (Eds.), *Kommunikationsmanagement (Loseblattwerk 2001 ff.): Vol. 124. Innovationskommunikation – Strategisches Handlungsfeld für Corporate Communications.* Neuwied: Luchterhand.

Zerfaß, A., Sandhu, S., & Huck, S. (2004b). Kommunikation von Innovationen – Neue Ideen und Produkte erfolgreich positionieren. *Kommunikationsmanager, 1*(2), 56–58. Retrieved from http://www.communicationcontrolling.de/fileadmin/_innovate/downloads/kommunikation_von_innovationen.pdf

Inga Haase since 2015 is a researcher at the Chair for SME Management and Entrepreneurship at the University of Siegen where she completed her doctorate with summa cum laude in 2017. She wrote her thesis on communication in open innovation processes of small enterprises. After finishing her studies in business management at the University of Siegen in 2009, she worked as an Innovation Manager and Right Hand of the Management in a German SME. Her primary research interests are innovation, communication, and embeddedness in the context of SMEs and entrepreneurship. She has already presented her research at several international conferences.

Open Innovation in a Start-up Firm

Lura Rexhepi Mahmutaj and Besnik Krasniqi

Abstract Growth, success and survival depend on the capability of the firms to innovate and network continuously. The purpose of this book chapter is to explore the impact of open innovation in the start-up firm growth. SMEs are capable to develop innovation, but not many of them are able to manage the whole innovation process. This implies the need for collaboration of SMEs with others, such as other firms or academic and research institutions. The research approach is based on a single case study by interviewing an innovative firm in Kosovo, Formon 3D Printer. The empirical findings show a low level of open innovation with establishment of Formon 3D. They managed to collaborate with only one professor of University of Prishtina at the beginning stage. Indeed, open innovation has its crucial importantly, especially for start-ups in transition countries. Yet, challenges to effective collaboration still remain as entrepreneurs often question their partners' commitment to supporting firm growth. This study provides findings valid for innovative private firms in Kosovo, and should not be generalized to other firms in Kosovo, the region or beyond.

Introduction

Growth, success and survival depend on the capability of the firms to innovate and network continuously (Varis and Littunen 2010). Innovation is an important factor for organizational survival and growth (Pullen et al. 2009); nevertheless, SMEs are characterized by greater uncertainty and dependence on their environment due to their small size and market share (Fadahunsi 2012), as well as lack of resources for growth and the expected business risks (Pasanen 2007). Yet SMEs tend to overcome these obstacles due to their flexibility, innovation development, and networks (Fadahunsi 2012).

L. R. Mahmutaj · B. Krasniqi (✉)
Faculty of Economics, University of Prishtina "Hasan Prishtina", Prishtina, Kosovo
e-mail: lura.rexhepi@uni-pr.edu; besnik.krasniqi@uni-pr.edu

© Springer Nature Switzerland AG 2019   109
G. Rexhepi et al. (eds.), *Open Innovation and Entrepreneurship*,
https://doi.org/10.1007/978-3-030-16912-1_7

In the recent years, there has been a growing interest among academics about the importance of innovation and networks in firms' performance. Nevertheless, few studies have examined its effectiveness through innovation and networks. To fill this gap, this research study aims to explore the impact of innovation in business performance and its linkage with networking.

New technologies are becoming extremely powerful to gain competitive advantage, as well as commercial success for firms among different sectors. This complexity goes beyond the skills and capabilities of individual firms, which forces them to start creating relationships with different firms and institutions to lessen the burden of uncertainties related to novel products (Hagedoorn and Duysters 2002). Strategic technology alliances involve inter-firm cooperation for combined innovative activity or technology exchange, which are expected to have mutual benefit. The innovative capability has to do with a specific expertise in related to the introduction of novel products and/or processes (Hagedoorn and Duysters 2002). In this book chapter, the researchers focus on the role of open innovation in new product commercialization in 3D printing technology as an illustration. To create value for customers and anticipate new market opportunities, assets and competencies from different actors should be linked which will lead to inter-organizational network.

Interorganizational networks are associated with the idea of open innovation. This is because the most important reason why firms are cooperating with each other is the technological complexity. Chesbrough (2003a) highlights that traditional model of innovation is becoming obsolete because it was mainly internally focused. The new paradigm is open innovation, which is largely focused on internal and external sources of ideas, going through multiple paths, such as extensive field research, academic study and others. Open innovation is about enlightening the role for R&D, proper management and access to intellectual property, as well as achieve firm growth. This book chapter is structured in the following way. First, the researchers explore some evolutions in the 3D Printing and analyze how companies create network value and create competitive advantage in the market. The next section explains how value constellations create value in start-up firms. Start-up firms that launch radical innovative products based on new technologies use different business models by identifying the maximum value creation through network, as well as identifying external resources that have to be generated from various partners. The next section examines open innovation benefits for start-ups. This chapter concludes with implications for companies and some possible avenues for further research.

Literature Review

Value Creation in Value Constellations

New technologies offer opportunities to create value constellations with the purpose of offering new products based on new business models (Christensen 1997; Christensen and Raynor 2003). It should be mention that value creation is at the center of business strategy. In value creating system, every partner occupies a specific position with the aim to add value to input before passing to the other actor within the system (Porter 1985). Moreover, actors within value-creating system produce value by rethinking the roles and interrelationships (Ramirez and Wallin 2000). It is important to calculate benefits from the network value creation in order to ensure that each participant is satisfied and stay committed to the network.

The notion of Open Innovation can be better understood by value constellations. This is because it requires combination of proper assets and competencies to be tied for value constellation. There is also a need to have governance mode between partners through any collaborative agreement in order to commercialize an innovation. The coordination modes may vary also on the level of control and coordination need for the innovation in order to ensure that quality and technological specifications are delivered to customers (Chesbrough 2003a). Moreover, Resource-Based View theory helps to understand open innovation because of the bundling of unique resources.

Stabell and Fjeldstad (1998) highlight the importance of value creation of networks characterized by actual and potential relationships among different actors. Value network helps companies to define the types of networks which enable innovation development. The current shift from closed to open innovation is about creating value network with various partners for innovation to better respond to customer, needs and expectations; react to competitors and strives for firm success (Christensen 1997). The idea of open innovation identifies several actors as partners, including R&D experts, to create new business models, leading to financial value creation (Chesbrough 2003a; Christensen 1997). The duration of the relationships created among firms may last within weeks or even years, depending different circumstances.

Open Innovation

In the past, firms were competing with each other on how much they invested in R&D and protected intellectual property from spilling over. It was believed that through this approach, they will be able to innovate faster, achieving competitive advantage. This is called closed innovation paradigm, which is about having aggressive control over internal knowledge to avoid from leaking outside (Herzog and Leker 2010). Nevertheless, this paradigm has been challenged because of the increase in the number of knowledge workers and private venture capital (Chesbrough 2003a). In this way, firms encounter difficulty to control R&D investments, as if innovative ideas fall outside the operations of firms, then they can be commercialized by knowledge workers by establishing start-up firm. New firms can commercialize innovative ideas within market through private venture capital (Chesbrough 2006). Moreover, firms can obtain new innovative solutions by bringing problems to knowledge workers, and have them spin off innovative ideas or solutions to other firms through intermediaries (Boudreau and Lakhani 2009). This new paradigm is called open innovation which has increased attention among practitioners and researchers (Enkel et al. 2009).

Globalization and technological advancements has been challenging for many firms; thus, to cope with environmental changes, many of them are adopting open innovation strategy as they cannot use only internal R&D for innovation in this world with distributed knowledge (Rohrbeck et al. 2009). The main reason for this is because firms that try to be too internally focused might miss innovative opportunities that need to combine external technologies (Chesbrough 2003b). Keupp and Gassmann (2009) highlight that firms should not rely at high extent in their internal measures, considering the high costs of internal R&D and financial risks of innovation. To share this uncertainty and risk, firms need to consider co-creation of innovation through partnership. Thus, it is better for firms to focus on external sources of knowledge to sustain innovation and firm growth (Laursen and Salter 2006).

According to Chesbrough (2003a), open innovation had been analysed at the firm level in the past, specifically from point of view of technology user. Now, open innovation is considered the relationships between partners through equity or non-equity alliances, corporate venturing investments, etc. (Bamford et al. 2003). It includes strategic alliances, and it is about deciding on how to select partners, assess the benefits and risks from the network, ensure fit between different partners, as well as develop a cooperative agreement between them. Key innovating companies are the ones who manage interorganizational networks to develop new technologies, as well as to exploit technology based on market needs. It is crucial for key players of open innovation to find interesting partners, manage networks efficiently and use appropriate measures to minimize tensions between partners (Vanhaverbeke and Cloodt 2005).

In this dynamic environment, firms encounter many challenges related to changes in customer preferences, and often their preferences are not well understood; thus, innovation approaches should be established by cooperating with external parties (Boudreau and Lakhani 2009). There are different benefits of open innovation. Firms can obtain an advances technology and complement internal innovation activities when they cooperate with external parties (Lichtenthaler 2008). Also, when firms become a part of strategic ventures, they are able to leverage innovation capabilities, spread the innovation risk among collaborators and share its uncertainty (Keupp and Gassmann 2009). In this manner, firms can lower the cost of innovation by obtaining knowledge and expertise in different areas from partners (Chesbrough 2006). Moreover, to improve acceptance of products to customers, firms should collaborate also with customers and suppliers (Von Hippel 2001).

The importance of having network has been found in the field of innovation theory, as well. Network means ties created between independent entities from each other. Organizations, which are part of network usually have higher rate of innovation. There are long-term benefits which firms intend to receive; thus, they become part of a network. Some of the benefits of network comprise of an increase in the market share, total sale, and in the number of employees (Havnes and Senneseth 2001). Some other benefits from network include higher turnover, profit rates and expansion of product range (Gardet and Mothe 2012). SMEs have utilized efficiently external networks, leading to shorter innovation time, lower risk and cost; as well as increase in the flexibility of their operation (Lee et al. 2010). The diversity of individuals and firms with unique skills and capabilities is one the main benefits, as they are able to better exploit new innovations. An illustration can be working closely with customers, where SMEs may identify opportunities for improvements and receive new innovation thoughts and create customers' value (Chetty and Stangl 2010).

On the other hand, there are firms who encounter difficulties in profiting from open innovation. Some firms faced challenges to open up their product development to external partners, as well as managing such innovation. This is because it is crucial to find the right partner who can contribute as a valuable knowledge source for innovation (Boudreau and Lakhani 2009). Moreover, many firms struggle to balance resources between open innovation activities and internal R&D, considering the scare resources within firms (Enkel et al. 2009). On the other hand, if managed successfully, radical innovation can be developed by combination of external knowledge which is beneficial for the long run (March 1991). Another challenge can be that connecting to various partners through open innovation does not guarantee successful innovation and superior growth (Laursen and Salter 2006). Moreover, West and Gallagher (2006) claim that firms which were successful with closed innovation tend to see themselves as superior to competitors; thus, does not cooperate with others. Indeed, it is crucial to understand mechanisms for open innovation in order to achieve intended benefits among partners. On way can be through license-in outside technology or intellectual property to complement internal activities of innovation (Lichtenthaler 2008), which lead to obtaining competitive advantage in the market (Dodgson et al. 2006). This is about knowledge transfer from vendors to clients, which complements absorptive capacity created by internal R&D (Cohen and Levinthal 1990). Gray (2006) argue that absorptive capacity includes also overall capacity for learning, implementing and disseminating new knowledge inside the firm, as well as using new resources as technologies. Absorptive capacity is able to successfully replicate new knowledge (Ahimbisibwe et al. 2016). SMEs that have a high level of absorptive capacity are considered to be more proactive (Huston and Sakkab 2006). An example can be when Apple Computer used licencing-in of the graphical user interface (GUI) technology from Xerox (Chesbrough 2003b). Another mechanism for open innovation involves strategic alliances with suppliers and competitors, which allows them to exploit opportunities and respond to market and technological change by using core competencies from network partners (Xie and Johnston 2004). Inter-firm collaboration is important to have cooperation between firms with common goals. An illustration can be a strategic alliance of dedicated biotechnology companies and large, integrated pharmaceutical companies (Grant and Baden-Fuller 2004). Moreover, open networks is another mechanism that helps firms to find solution to their problems through seekers. Through open networks, firms post a problem, and wait for solutions within a certain deadline. Then firms or solvers from different disciplines and variety of professional knowledge tackle these problems to receive incentives. An illustration

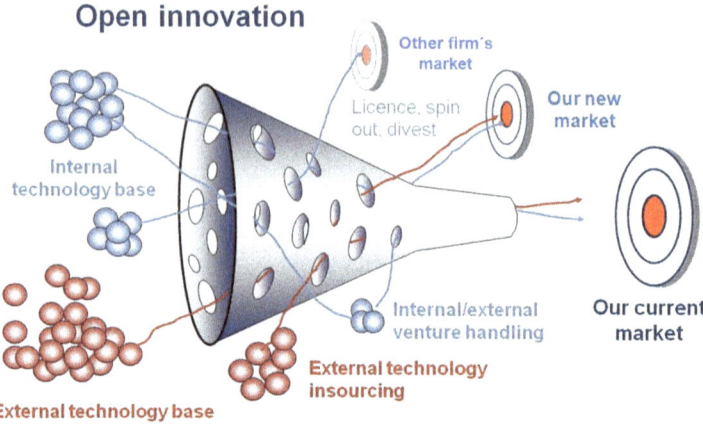

Fig. 1 Open innovation. Source: Chesbrough 2006

for this is Innovation Exchange.com that functions in way which matches firms seeking innovation products, services or processes with individual experts or firms offering such innovation. Nevertheless, it is crucial that solvers sign a contract related to confidentiality and intellectual property rights, while seekers pay the agreed amount for the problem solved (Boudreau and Lakhani 2009).

The following Fig. 1 describes Open innovation, and the parties involved in it. This is an open business model, which combines internal and external ideas, as well as paths to market in order to advance technologies (Chesbrough 2006).

Small and Medium Enterprises in Kosovo

The Kosovo's transitional path from centrally planned to a market economy, interrupted by conflict, occupation, and War (1998–1999), which have influenced the pathway of private sector and economic development of the country. Kosova is amongst poorest European countries with GDP per capita of 2800 Euros generated from services (56%), industry 18%, agriculture 17%, and construction 10%. Deindustrialization marked by the shrink of industry share of GDP (47% 1989 to 15% during early stage of the post conflict period) influenced heavy imbalances in macroeconomic configuration. Trade deficit reaching about 40% of GDP and unemployment rate above 30% are key problems (Krasniqi 2012).

The private sector and entrepreneurship begin to develop in the beginning of 1990s. The growth in the number of new businesses took place between 1991 and 1993 when the number of private firms tripled. This period of the rapid growth was followed by a period of stagnation as perhaps the social and political conditions deteriorated and declined in 1998, when the occupation started to manifest in its extreme form. In the aftermath of the War, (1999) the sharp increase in the number of business start-ups took place. The total number of registered businesses in 2003 was 49,874, and experienced huge increase thereafter by reaching 159,724 in 2016 (Agency for Business Registration 2017). Majority of private companies are SMEs suggesting that private sector consists entirely on small firms (Krasniqi and Mustafa 2016; Lajqi and Krasniqi 2017). On the type of business ownership, majority of businesses are organized as individual businesses. According to the Agency for Business Registration (ABR) in 2016, 85% of enterprises were registered as individual. The low value added and export potential of the private sector remains a concern for development suggesting the need for supporting innovation in SMEs (Kotorri and Krasniqi 2018).

Building innovation capacities of SMEs remains a challenge for private sector development. There is a need for further improvement in terms of other support services to develop skills base of SMEs and start-ups. Although, Kosovo, made some progress according to the SBA Policy Index 2016 it needs to make a more sustained effort to build knowledge and skills among SMEs which keen to trade with the EU. The OECD report on Innovation System in Kosovo (2013) found that innovation in businesses tends to be driven by external competitive pressures and customer requirements with most of entrepreneurs considering diaspora as source of knowledge transfer. This may signal that cooperation with diaspora would potentially form the basis for more exploitation of open innovation in Kosovo (see Krasniqi and Williams 2018).

On the policy environment for innovation there is much to be done. The Research and Innovation, the Economic Reform Programme 2017–2019 (ERP) states that, Kosovo's capacity for research, development and innovation (RDI) is very low, this limits the creation of new jobs. The ERP (GoK 2016) recognises and points out the lack of a legal and policy framework as well as the low level of political commitment to RDI, which is reflected in the very low public expenditure (0.1% of GDP). The analysis also adequately signals the lack of incentives for the private sector and academia, although there is no reference to the companies' low absorption capacity and universities' limited capacity for specialised research and lack of results in commercialisation. The measure to improve the policy and strategic framework is new but the expected impact may not be achieved if the measure is not complemented by more ambitious actions to assist and boost applied research activities in Higher Education, and to substantially improve cooperation between research institutions and private sector. The case study in this chapter will show how the innovative SMEs could benefit from qualified experts from academia.

SMEs and Open Innovation

In the small firms, value networks provide them with interesting opportunities considering that they are characterized by scarce resources. Value networks help them to use the core competencies of small firms in a wider context. The access to value networks for small firms depends on the ability of the entrepreneur personal contacts and relationships (Thorelli 1986). There is a gap in the existing literature about the SMEs value networks. Blankenburg-Holm et al. (1999) argues that before creating value, network parties should follow four stages, such as value creation followed by the initial business connection, mutual commitment and mutual dependence. The role of entrepreneurs in early stages of network is dominated until the last stage of mutual dependence, which includes intertwined business processes of the co-operating businesses. The role of entrepreneurs in value network become more strategic, thus it is more manageable. Nevertheless, firm innovation capability decreases; thus, there is a need for external support (Howells 2006). For instance, network facilitation supports setting objectives, as well as mutual learning, which helps SME networks to grow beyond their social networks (Harding 2002). To create new value and exploit new opportunities, participating firms in a network should share a joint understanding or shared commitment for joint action (Blankenburg-Holm et al. 1999). Other authors agree that SMEs need to engage in creating networking value, because it is extremely difficult for them to introduce innovation by themselves (Gruenberg-Bochard and Kreis-Hoyer 2009; Jørgensen and Ulhøi 2010). Value networks are opportunity driven, and it is necessary to evaluate partners' ability to deliver value to the network. In this manner, all partners can evaluate benefits received from joint actions and decide whether it is worth to continue in a specific network (Kothandaraman and Wilson 2001).

Even though SMEs are capable to introduce innovation, not many of them are able to manage the whole process. This shows a necessity to establish cooperation of SMEs with other partners, such as other firms or academic and research institutions, to promote innovation capabilities and achieve competitive advantage in the market (Konsti-Laakso et al. 2012). The open innovation term was used firstly by large technology-based companies due to their larger resources; yet, it can be applied to SMEs by introducing innovations and increasing their technological competences through inter-firm cooperation (Lee et al. 2010). Combining various knowledge and assets is the main benefit by participating different actors (Konsti-Laakso et al. 2012). Marketing agency which contributes in innovation process and cooperate intensely through market exploitation, market test or customer needs analysis is an illustration of open innovation (Lee et al. 2010). The next section proceeds with a detailed description of the evolution of 3D Printing technology, and discusses the research methodology used to conduct this study, which is based on single case study research approach.

The Evolution of 3D Printing, Case Study of Formon

The Evolution of 3D Printing

3D printing technology was invented in the year of 1980, which has been evolved gradually to fit the needs of the customers. Nowadays, this technology made it likely to print models with different kind of materials, such as metals, metal alloys, and thermoplastic, thermoplastic composites and ceramic. The highest sold 3D printers in United States in 2014 was industrial grade 3D Printers, which shows that industries are abandoning the old ways of doing things, and are embracing this technology in their work (Wordpress 2017). 3D printing is considered different from machinery processes, as its systems join raw materials to develop an object. From 3D printing can be build physical models, prototypes, patterns, tooling components or production parts. These machines have been largely sold to R&D based firms that require high quality objects, which afford premium price. Various industrial 3D printing systems are offered by more than thirty 3D printing companies around the world. Recently, 3D printing manufacturers started to target lower end of the market by offering more affordable machines in order to make a viable option also for small businesses, engineers and designers, schools and individual consumers (de Jong and de Bruijn 2013).

3D printing is applied in different fields, and the following present two examples in medical and manufacturing fields. In medical field, 3D printing has brought big changes; it has made possible organ and tissue fabrication (skin grafting), as well as the creation of implant model and pharmaceutical research. Another contribution of 3D printing in this field comprises of personalization and customization of medical equipment which is more effective, and improves quality and quantity of production (Wordpress 2017). 3D Printing has been also applicable for hearing aids and dental implants (de Jong and de Bruijn 2013). On the other hand, one of the fastest growing areas of 3D production is in manufacturing industry (Wordpress 2017). It can be used in manufacturing organizations for product parts in the consumer, industrial, medical and military markets (de Jong and de Bruijn 2013). The cost of 3D printing is high, but it is decreasing because of the evolution of the printers, where manufacturing field can use to produce various products with the assistance of 3D printing. It is crucial for industrial enterprises to assess their operations in order to increase the quality of the products they are producing. Indeed, the usage of 3D printing technology is considered to be a transformative tool in different field (Wordpress 2017).

The following are some illustrations of how can 3D printing technology benefit firms in long term. Designers are able to operate more efficiently and save time with the use of this technology, as they can prototype various designs to test their viability. Another usage is in manufacturing products or products parts that would be very expensive with traditional production line. Also, it is used in production, logistics and retail, since individuals can download and print the product's design (de Jong and de Bruijn 2013).

Open Source 3D Printing Technology

3D Printing has been seen as transformative technology. There is a recent evolution of this technology, and it is crucial that top executives in the firms understand the changing phase of technological innovation. There is emergence of open-source 3D printing, which needs to be examined and fit to general trend of open innovation by developing collaborative innovation projects (de Jong and de Bruijn 2013).

Users began to collaborate in order to develop home printer designs and share in the Web their open-source designs, which have stimulated to develop a community for open-source 3D printing. Some examples of user-founded companies are Bits From Bytes, based in Clevedon, United Kingdom; Makerbot Industries, based in Brooklyn, New York; and Ultimaking Ltd., based in Geldermalsen, the Netherlands, who are focused on lower-end market segment of 3D printing. It should be highlighted that these companies (open-source printers) represent a challenge to existing 3D printer companies (de Jong and de Bruijn 2013).

The emerging phenomenon of open collaborative innovation is considered the growth of open-source 3D printing. This way of collaboration involves contributors sharing their work of generating a design, including outputs from individual and collective design efforts, which are open to use for everyone. Even though open-source communities have been developed mostly for software development, they can be used also to introduce also physical products. This has been popularized because of the transition to digitized design and production practices, along with internet-based communication which involves low cost to engage in innovation activities. These collaboration innovation initiatives can happen in nascent industries, which involve not served potential users, as well as industries where not all users are served (de Jong and de Bruijn 2013).

Nascent industries are emerging new industries, where user communities innovate and use their new products before commercial production. They justify their investments based on expected benefits that they will receive from innovation. It can be concluded that users firstly innovate for themselves, then for communities, and when they are aware that the demand is certain, then commercial production is seen as feasible. For instance, Strtasys, which is a 3D manufacturer, started to make only a toy frog for his daughter using glue gun by mixing polyethylene and candle wax. This was an innovation trigger to automate the process and invent new innovation which was 3D printing technology (de Jong and de Bruijn 2013). Moreover, user communities had potential to develop also in existing industries where some potential users are not served at all. This situation is dedicated to the products targeted to the high-end users who are able to afford high prices that to overcome firms' initial investments costs. For instance, cell phones were mostly sold to big customers, and only after the technology has sufficiently matured, medium-sized and small firms, followed by individual end customers were served. On the other hand, there might be cases when customers are not served well. An example can be the case of 3D printing where cheaper systems that are viable for all customers are being served, such as the case of RepRap community that has filled this market gap (de Jong and de Bruijn 2013).

Case Study Method

As identified in the Literature Review, research in open innovation and SMEs is still at an early stage, and there is much scope for exploratory studies in this area. This research adopts qualitative approach to analyze the topic of open innovation. Single case study method has been used in order to capture experiences and attitudes of people on how they perceive an issue (McCusker and Gunaydin 2015). Semi-structure interview with an innovative firm from Kosovo called Formon has been used as systematic approach to ensure that the main questions are covered, to change the sequence of questions when needed, as well as to ask sub-question to clarify and elaborate issues more deeply related to open innovation (Ritchie and Lewis 2003). The researchers have looked at firms' documentary materials, newspaper interviews, the social media, as well as their website. To analyze documents properly and crosscheck information collected through the interview, this approach ensured research accuracy (Forster 1994).

When using single case study, it is important to be able to explore the case, as well as be capable to understand the context of important issue in order to possess rich insights. Other benefits of using single case study are that they are less expensive and not time-consuming compared to multiple case studies. This research approach helps the researcher to get deeper understanding of exploring specific subject (Yin 2003). Nevertheless, there are critics of this research approach among academics embracing a positivist mindset. For them, adoption of statistical methods is the most reliable approach, and case study approach has limitation on ensuring objectivity (Donmoyer 1990; Yin 2009). The main limitation of single case study approach is the lack of external validity, as the results cannot be generalized at high extent (Yin 2009).

Company Profile: FORMON

3D printers are a type of industrial robot that is able to print 3D models using successive layers of material. 3D Printer has started to be developed in the US; nevertheless, in Europe, there are few companies that sell such products. This is new industry with high potentials for growth. Formon exploited this opportunity to develop a differentiated product in order to penetrate in international market. This is the hardware product, and they are the first company that launched such product in Balkan. They were inspired also from Sony Company from Japan, as Japan was perceived not so high developed by others in the world, but when they developed Sony products with high technology, the perception has changed as a more developed country. So they believe that they can offer such product as well in Kosovo. They were invited also in Turkey to develop this company completely; nevertheless, they wanted to do it here in Kosovo.

Formon believes that making lies at the core of humanity. That's how they built civilizations and that's how they are going to build the future. The age of our employees is from 24 to 28 years old. Our products are designed and engineered for a remarkable making experience. They are designed for all the architects, designers, engineers and any 3D printing enthusiasts and beginners. The company is founded on the premise of bringing the magic of 3D printing on every desk. They are certified with ISO 9001:2015 for quality management system.

3D Printing is very new product in Europe as well. They are in process of certifying with CE, which is costly. They have three direct competitors in Europe: makerboot in USA, Ultimaker (Netherlands) and Davinci (Poloni). Nevertheless, their price is much higher around 1500.00 to 3700.00 euros, while Formon is trying to sell these printers with 599.00 euros in the international market. To use other printers, there is a need to learn through training about its usage as well as about the maintenance. What Formon has done with their printer, they have automatize all that process. There are three things that make Formon more competitive: lower price, simpler usage, and quality for which also provide warranty for 2 years. It is used by people who design different products; for example architectural firms seize more opportunities by creating complex, durable models in-house. A 3D printer can create any object for you to convince your client with one, or several high quality models during your pitch. 3D printers are used to create low-cost architectural models used as study models during the creation process. 3D printers are used to build realistic and detailed architectural models, often used to promote a project by showcasing the final result in 3D, in a visually striking way. If architects have spent about 1 month to do mock-ups (maketa), now they can do for 24 hours to complete the mock-up, and they print it the same way as you print a letter in a printer. Until now, Formon sold this product in Kosovo, Canada, England, Serbia, and Albania. They sold about 42 3D printers that were delivered to clients, and they have ordered 68 other printers, where most of them will be distributed to schools. They didn't do marketing at all, only through PR and application for innovation awards, such as Albanian ICT Awards—Innovation of the year 2015; FIDES Philanthropy Awards—Innovation Award; Foundcenter Investment "CATCH" challenge—Innovation Award and A' Design Award and Competition Winner of Prosumer Products, Tools, and Machinery Design Category, 2016–2017. All these awards contributed to talk about them from different newspapers in the region. Nevertheless, when Formon penetrates their product in Europe, they would also develop a marketing campaign in order to have fast growth. They will start to spread their product in retail stores in Germany firstly, and then will continue to other places as well.

In order to get deep understanding of this start-up firm, the researchers interviewed one of the co-owner. The interview guide consisted of six parts, such as dealing with suppliers, their cooperation level for innovation, financial support, intellectual property rights, ISO standards and organizational innovation culture, which are described in the following.

Dealing with Suppliers
Formon was established by starting everything from scratch. To develop the first product 3D printer, they encountered difficulties to find suppliers and this took about 1.5 years to find the right ones and create trust in relationship. Also, it took time to test different parts. This experience improved their skills and capabilities of dealing communicating and finding suitable suppliers; thus, it has shorten time in about 50% in relationship with another product which is conceptually designed with other technology, and which is almost ready for the market. It also provided great lessons to have better and faster collaboration with suppliers for the next product. At the

beginning, they have done many prototypes until they came to the final product. In the future, they aim to develop two prototypes, so the third one to be the final product.

Cooperation

The product has three parts: electronic engineering, software engineering, and hardware engineering. In general, the professors of University of Prishtina were not so collaborative, considering that they didn't believe in their capability to develop such product. Professors were willing to meet them, but so much advice was provided to them. Nevertheless, they managed to collaborate with a professor of University of Prishtina, who explained some complex formulas needed to develop 3D printer technology.

Financial Support

The following are some companies that have assisted financially for this product: Help, ICK, Raiffaisen, FIQ, USAID, Helvetas, USAID and IPKO Foundation. For instance, Help (Germany) bought them some machines that were needed of electronic tiles; and ICK has provided infrastructure: using their office space to conduct business.

Intellectual Property Rights

Formon received trademark and industrial design in Kosovo, and in Europe they are in the process of getting them. In Kosovo, they encountered challenge because of the complex procedures and inadequate staff, who have not been capable to inform and instruct about the procedure of applying for trademark and industrial design. To penetrate in Europe, they are collaborating with a company for the application to get the patent in the World Property Office, and they are in the final process to receive it.

ISO Standards

They possess ISO 9001 (2015) for development, producing and sales of product.

Organizational Innovation Culture

Empirical results from a single case study show that there is moderate innovative culture within Formon. Their organizational culture is developed in such a way, that employees are encouraged and have the obligations to discuss about their work challenges during the day, which helps them to come up with new innovative ideas and improve products and services given to clients. Nevertheless, they do not have internal innovation proposal policy to reward employees with bonuses, as at this stage, they are not grown to afford this kind of measures. Moreover, at Formon, employees get employed and they are engaged immediately in projects. Their organization is also used as a platform, when the students graduate from engineering field, and they have a place to express their talents.

All these dimensions helped the researchers to gain understanding of the level of open innovation that can be developed within start-up innovative firm in transition firms, such as Kosovo.

Discussion and Conclusions

The concept of open innovation has been very popular in the recent years. Open innovation is growing and it is influencing technological change. Open innovation is serving to search and solve various problems of innovations. The shift from closed to open innovation has increased opportunities to connect technology markers. Efficient negotiations among partners should be developed to have successful open innovation. Some of the benefits of open innovation include facilitation of internal and external technology commercialization, connection between seekers and providers of innovation, as well as share of risks and benefits among partners (Hossain 2012). 3D printing technology is a process of developing three-dimensional solid object, which is used for prototyping and distributed manufacturing, applied different fields (Patent iNSIGHT Pro and PatSeer 2014). There is an important role of innovative user communities in the market, as they can be proactive and reveal features that existing industries are lacking. Also, they can offer cheaper products that fulfill customers' needs. The emergence of open source 3D printers shows that innovation by user communities is productive because of improved understanding of modular design practices, lower design and collaboration costs due to the cheaper and more capable computerized design tools, lower communication costs due to the access to Internet, and more educated populations of citizens around the world (de Jong and de Bruijn 2013).

Although limited, open innovation for Formon was very beneficial. Formon has cooperated with a professor from University of Prishtina. They have received financial support from different institutions. Nevertheless, they are having difficulties to cope with costs associated coming from intellectual property rights, especially to receive a patent from World Property Office. This start-up should develop open innovation at higher extent. They should look for different ways to find suitable external partners, with whom they could share the benefits and risks associated to open innovation and penetrate faster in the international market.

An innovative firm of 3D printing in Kosovo, Formon, is single case study used in this research. Similar to RepRap community, they have developed this product to offer at cheaper price, and their aim is to penetrate in international market. They have started as a user community described in the literature with the role of introducing innovation and gain profits. Open innovation was used by this company, but at lesser degree, considering that they have cooperated only with a professor from University of Prishtina. One of the implications from this research for Formon firm is that because of numerous advantages of open innovation, they should search for new ways of collaboration with external partners even if they are outside Kosovo, because the expected benefits are higher than the costs associated with this development. This will help penetrate faster at international market and achieve higher firm growth rates.

The empirical results are in line with the literature review highlighting the importance of collaborating with universities when introducing an innovation (Chetty and Stangl 2010). Bianchi et al. (2010) shows the importance of open innovation in SMEs growth, seeing it as a solution to overcome challenges related to scarce resources, lack of skilled employees and financial constraints. Other authors agree that the main obstacles to innovation for SMEs are financial constraints, lack of skilled labor, lack of networks and collaboration (Laforet and Tann 2006). When firms are part of a network, there have higher chances to expand in the market, as well as increase their size and sales (Havnes and Senneseth 2001). Chesbrough (2006) highlight that open innovation for small firms makes it much easier to share technology and IP with other partners. They need to protect their innovation with IP in order not to be copied by others. In transition countries, open innovation has crucial importance for SMEs. To be successfully developed, government policies should be developed to initiate process of communication and collaboration, as well as monitoring it. Open innovation should bring innovative goods and services which fulfill market needs in transition countries. The communication costs are very cheap considering the availability of access to Internet; thus, building network should be a starting point for innovative firms. Nevertheless, considering that there is a lack of research centers, infrastructure and universities in many developing countries; as well as open innovation is still a new concept among SMEs, more research studies should be done in this field (Vrgovic et al. 2012).

References

Agency for Business Registration. (2017). *Basic performance indicators for business registration in Kosovo*. Retrieved from https://arbk.rks-gov.net/desk/inc/media/F1D24200-80B8-4255-BDD7-12F833FDC97D.pdf

Ahimbisibwe, G. M., Nkundabanyanga, S. K., Nkurunziza, G., & Nyamuyonjo, D. (2016). Knowledge absorptive capacity: Do all its dimensions matter for export performance of SMEs? *World Journal of Entrepreneurship, Management and Sustainable Development, 12*(2), 139–160.

Bamford, J., Gomes-Casseres, B., & Robinson, M. (2003). *Mastering alliance strategy: A comprehensive guide to design, management and organization*. San Francisco, CA: Jossey-Bass/Wiley.

Bianchi, M., Orto, S. C., Frattini, F., & Vercesi, P. (2010). Enabling open innovation in small- and medium-sized enterprises: How to find alternative applications for your technologies. *R and D Management, 40*(4), 414–430.

Blankenburg-Holm, D. B., Eriksson, K., & Johansson, J. (1999). Creating value through mutual commitment to business network relationships. *Strategic Management Journal, 20*, 467–486.

Boudreau, K. J., & Lakhani, K. R. (2009). How to manage outside innovation. *MIT Sloan Management Review, 50*(4), 69–76.

Chesbrough, H. (2003a). *Open innovation: The new imperative for creating and profiting from technology*. Boston, MA: Harvard Business School Press.

Chesbrough, H. (2003b). The era of open innovation. *MIT Sloan Management Review, 44*(3), 35–41.

Chesbrough, H. (2006). *Open business models: How to thrive in the new innovation landscape*. Boston, MA: Harvard Business School Press.

Chetty, S. K., & Stangl, L. M. (2010). Internationalization and innovation in a network relationship context. *European Journal of Marketing, 44*(11/12), 1725–1743.

Christensen, C. M. (1997). *The innovator's dilemma: When new technologies cause great firms to fail*. Boston, MA: Harvard Business School Press.

Christensen, C. M., & Raynor, M. E. (2003). *The innovator's solution: Creating and sustaining successful growth*. Boston, MA: Harvard Business School Press.

Cohen, W. M., & Levinthal, D. A. (1990). Absorptive capacity: A new perspective on learning and innovation. *Administrative Science Quarterly, 35*, 128–152.

de Jong, J. P., & de Bruijn, E. (2013). Innovative lessons in 3D printing. *MIT Sloan Management Review, 54*, 42–52.

Dodgson, M., Gann, D., & Salter, A. (2006). The role of technology in the shift towards open innovation: The case of Procter and Gamble. *R&D Management, 36*(3), 333–346.

Donmoyer, R. (1990). Generalizability and the single-case study. In E. W. Eisner & A. Peshkin (Eds.), *Qualitative inquiry in education: the continuing debate* (pp. 175–200). New York: Teachers College Press.

Enkel, E., Gassmann, O., & Chesbrough, H. (2009). Open R&D and open innovation: Exploring this phenomenon. *R&D Management, 39*(4), 311–316.

Fadahunsi, A. (2012). The growth of small businesses: Towards a research agenda. *American Journal of Economics and Business Administration, 4*(1), 105–115.

Forster, N. (1994). The analysis of company documentation. In C. Cassell & G. Symon (Eds.), *Qualitative methods in organisational research*. London: Sage.

Grant, R. M., & Baden-Fuller, C. (2004). A knowledge accessing theory of strategic alliances. *Journal of Management Studies, 41*(1), 61–84.

Gray, C. (2006). Absorptive capacity, knowledge management and innovation in entrepreneurial small firms. *International Journal of Entrepreneurial Behavior & Research, 12*(6), 345–360.

Gardet, E., & Mothe, C. (2012). SME dependence and coordination in innovation networks. *Journal of Small Business and Enterprise Development, 19*(2), 263–280.

Gruenberg-Bochard, J., & Kreis-Hoyer, P. (2009). Knowledge-networking capability in German SMEs: A model for empirical investigation. *International Journal of Technology Management, 45*, 364–379.

Hagedoorn, J., & Duysters, G. (2002). External appropriation of innovative capabilities: The choice between strategic partnering and mergers and acquisitions. *Journal of Management Studies, 39*, 167–188.

Harding, S. J. (2002). *A networking model supporting small and medium enterprises to develop new processes and products*. PhD thesis, University of Nottingham.

Havnes, P. A., & Senneseth, K. (2001). A panel study of firm growth among SMEs in Networks. *Small Business Economics, 16*(4), 293–302.

Herzog, P., & Leker, J. (2010). Open and closed innovation: Different innovation cultures for different strategies. *International Journal of Technology Management, 52*(3), 322–343.

Hossain, M. (2012). Performance and potential of open innovation intermediaries. *Procedia - Social and Behavioral Sciences, 58*, 754–764.

Howells, J. (2006). Intermediation and the role of intermediaries in innovation. *Research Policy, 35*, 715–728.

Huston, L., & Sakkab, N. (2006). Connect and develop: Inside Procter & Gamble's new model for innovation. *Harvard Business Review, 84*(3), 58–66.

Jørgensen, F., & Ulhøi, J. P. (2010). Enhancing innovation capacity in SMEs through early network relationships. *Creativity and Innovation Management, 19*, 397–404.

Keupp, M. M., & Gassmann, O. (2009). Determinants and archetype users of open innovation. *R&D Management, 39*(4), 331–341.

Konsti-Laakso, S., Pihkala, T., & Kraus, S. (2012). Facilitating SME innovation capability through business networking. *Creativity and Innovation Management, 21*(1), 93–105.

Kothandaraman, P., & Wilson, D. T. (2001). The future of competition: Value-creating networks. *Industrial Marketing Management, 30*, 379–389.

Kotorri, M., & Krasniqi, B. A. (2018). Managerial characteristics and export performance–empirical evidence from Kosovo. *South East European Journal of Economics and Business, 13*(2), 32–48.

Krasniqi, B. A. (2012). *Entrepreneurship and small business development in Kosova*. New York: Nova Science Publishers.

Krasniqi, B. A., & Mustafa, M. (2016). Small firm growth in a post-conflict environment: The role of human capital, institutional quality, and managerial capacities. *International Entrepreneurship Management Journal, 12*(4), 1165–1207.

Krasniqi, B. A., & Williams, N. (2018). Migration and intention to return: Entrepreneurial intentions of the diaspora in post-conflict economies. Forthcoming in Post-Communist Economies.

Laforet, S., & Tann, J. (2006). Innovative characteristics of small manufacturing firms. *Journal of Small Business and Enterprise Development, 13*(3), 363–387.

Lajqi, S., & Krasniqi, B. A. (2017). Entrepreneurial growth aspirations in challenging environment: The role of institutional quality, human and social capital. *Strategic Change, 26*(4), 385–401.

Laursen, K., & Salter, A. J. (2006). Open for innovation: The role of openness in explaining innovation performance among UK manufacturing firms. *Strategic Management Journal, 27,* 131–150.

Lee, S., Park, G., Yoon, B., & Park, J. (2010). Open innovation in SMEs – An intermediated network model. *Research Policy, 39*(2), 290–300.

Lichtenthaler, U. (2008). Open innovation in practice: An analysis of strategic approaches to technology transactions. *IEEE Transactions on Engineering Management, 55*(1), 148–157.

March, J. G. (1991). Exploration and exploitation in organizational learning. *Organization Science, 2*(1), 71–87.

McCusker, K., & Gunaydin, S. (2015). Research using qualitative, quantitative or mixed methods and choice based on the research. *Perfusion, 30*(7), 537–542.

Pasanen, M. (2007). SME growth strategies: Organic or non-organic? *Journal of Enterprising Culture, 15*(4), 317–338.

Patent iNSIGHT Pro & PatSeer. (2014). *3D printing technology insight report.* Retrieved from https://www.patentinsightpro.com/techreports/0214/Tech%20Insight%20Report%20-%203D%20Printing.pdf

Porter, M. (1985). *Competitive advantage: Creating and sustaining superior performance.* New York: Free Press.

Pullen, A. J. J., De Weerd-Nederhof, P. C., Groen, A. J., Song, M., & Fisscher, O. A. M. (2009). Successful patterns of internal SME characteristics leading to high overall innovation performance. *Creativity and Innovation Management, 18*(3), 209–223.

Ramirez, R., & Wallin, J. (2000). *Prime movers. Define your business or have someone define it against you.* Chichester: Wiley.

Ritchie, J., & Lewis, J. (Eds.). (2003). *Qualitative research practice.* London: Sage.

Rohrbeck, R., Hölzle, K., & Gemünden, H. G. (2009). Opening up for competitive advantage: How Deutsche Telekom creates an open innovation ecosystem. *R&D Management, 39*(4), 420–430.

Stabell, C. B., & Fjeldstad, Ø. D. (1998). Configuring value for competitive advantage: On chains, shops, and networks. *Strategic Management Journal, 19*(5), 413–437.

Thorelli, H. B. (1986). Networks: Between markets and hierarchies. *Strategic Management Journal, 7,* 37–51.

Vanhaverbeke, W., & Cloodt, M. (2005). Chapter 13: Open innovation in value networks. In *Open innovation: Researching a new paradigm.* Oxford: Oxford University Press. Retrieved from https://www.academia.edu/2008515/Open_innovation_in_value_networks

Varis, M., & Littunen, H. (2010). Types of innovation, sources of information and performance in entrepreneurial SMEs. *European Journal of Innovation Management, 13*(2), 128–154.

Von Hippel, E. (2001). Innovation by user communities: Learning from open-source software. *MIT Sloan Management Review, 42*(4), 82–86.

Vrgovic, P., Vidicki, P., Glassman, B., & Walton, A. (2012). Open innovation for SMEs in developing countries – An intermediated communication network model for collaboration beyond obstacles. *Innovations, 14*(3), 290–302.

West, J., & Gallagher, S. (2006). Challenges of open innovation: The paradox of firm investment in open source software. *R&D Management, 36*(3), 319–331.

Wordpress. (2017). *The technology of the future is the key to survival.* Retrieved from http://www.nanopack.org/the-evolution-of-3d-printing/

Xie, F. T., & Johnston, W. J. (2004). Strategic alliances: Incorporating the impact of e-business technological innovations. *The Journal of Business Industrial Marketing, 19*(3), 208.

Yin, R. K. (2003). *Case study research: Design and methods*. Thousand Oaks, CA: Sage.

Yin, R. K. (2009). *Case studies: Design and methods* (4th ed.). Thousand Oaks, CA: Sage.

Lura Rexhepi Mahmutaj is a PhD in Entrepreneurship and SME Management, holding double degree from University of Nice Sophia Antipolis and University St. Kliment Ohridski—Bitola. She has earned a Master of Science degree in Strategic Project Management (European) from Heriot Watt University, Politecnico Di Milano, and Umea University. Dr. Rexhepi—Mahmutaj has substantial experience in lecturing at the University of Prishtina from 2011. She has done a study visit in Nice Sophia Antipolis. She was as a Tuck fellow in Dartmouth through TLP in 2016. Moreover, she has realized teaching and training staff mobility in the framework of the Erasmus + KA107 Programme. Her areas of research interests include innovation and SMEs growth.

Besnik Krasniqi, a Fulbright Scholar, holds MA and PhD in Economics from Staffordshire University (UK). He teaches Small Business and Entrepreneurship at the University of Prishtina. His career spans teaching and research in entrepreneurship at Maastricht School of Management (NL), Indiana University (USA), University of Michigan (USA), and Université Nice Sophia Antipolis (France). His work in the area of entrepreneurship, SMEs, and transition economies appeared in international journals such as *Small Business Economics, International Entrepreneurship and Management Journal, International Journal of Entrepreneurial Behavior & Research, Economic Systems*, and *Post-Communist Economies*. Professor Krasniqi is Certified Management Consultant. He has been recognized for his contribution to lobbying for entrepreneurship-friendly policies and building innovation and small business support packages in Kosovo and Balkans.

Lightning Source UK Ltd.
Milton Keynes UK
UKHW020840050619

343912UK00002B/26/P